A Walk in the Park

D1738632

To my great father, James D'Arcy, and to Walt,
without whom I wouldn't have this wonderful story

A WALK IN THE PARK
Reflections from Disneyland's First Host

Published by
Bonaventure Press
Post Office Box 51961
Irvine, CA 92619-1961
USA
www.bonaventurepress.com

All rights reserved. No part of this book may be reproduced or transmitted in any form or by any means, electronic or mechanical, including photocopying, recording or by any information storage and retrieval system without written permission from the author, except for the inclusion of brief quotations in a review.

Copyright © 2018 by Robert W. D'Arcy

Edited by David Koenig
Foreword by Judy Keigley

Library of Congress Cataloging-in-Publication Data
Library of Congress Control Number: 2018965643

A Walk in the Park: Reflections from Disneyland's First Host / by Bob D'Arcy;
foreword by Judy Keigley; editor, David Koenig
p. cm.
Includes index.

1. D'Arcy, Robert W., 1933 -
2. Disneyland (Calif.) — History.

ISBN 978-1-937878-09-2 (Softcover)

Manufactured in the United States of America

A Walk in the Park

Reflections from Disneyland's First Host

By Bob D'Arcy

BONAVENTURE PRESS

Acknowledgments

I would like to acknowledge some dear friends and family members who were instrumental in the making of my book, beginning with Rik Sivula, who is an avid reader and gave my book its first critical read and honest evaluation, followed by a big "thumbs up."

I would also like to acknowledge Michael Oletta, a fine photographer, who digitized my original photographs from film that I took during the construction of "The Site."

Of course, I must give a big thanks to my dear daughter, Erin De Maio, and another good friend, Wilma Sisbarro, for connecting me with Judy Marsh's daughter, whom I affectionately refer to as "Judy Love."

And to Judy Keigley ("Judy Love"), who reunited me with my sweetheart, her mother, after so many years apart, and who wrote the beautiful foreword to my book.

To my great friend Mike Buchta, a high school English teacher, I sincerely appreciate the time you spent in editing my book's initial rough draft and offering your criticisms.

The difficult and time-consuming task of entering my handwritten manuscript into a word processor, making it digital, was taken on by Carol McDonald. Thank you.

To my good friend and partner Daryl Wilson, who helped me to get connected with the right people to get this book published, set up my website and Facebook page (facebook.com/mr.bobdarcy), and kept the wheels greased until this book was well on its way to becoming a reality. I don't believe I could have gotten this far without you. Many thanks.

Finally, to my publisher and a wonderful man, David Koenig, who saw potential in my manuscript, put it into the professionally bound form it is today, and was instrumental in helping to promote both myself and my book.

Foreword

By Judy Keigley

Daughter of Judy Marsh,
The Original Slue Foot Sue

This book is a love story. The love of a cultural phenomenon and the love between a woman and a man; all told by a writer who has always chosen to walk in the world with love being his guiding light.

It is an honor to be asked to write a small contribution for this book.

What I believe makes this book so unique is how forthright it was written. Bob strips the Magical Kingdom of our imaginations and breaks it down to the bare bones of a man with a dream. In this

MY "JUDY LOVE," Judy Keigley, daughter of Judy Marsh

book, we get to know "Walt" as a person. We get to feel the magic of Disney from its beginning stages and follow the development as it becomes alive. Its first breaths are evident in its architecture, the pride of its employees and the steadfast vision of creating "The Happiest Place on Earth".

This behind the scenes perspective lets us in on the personal side of Disneyland, which only a few privileged people know. Disneyland has always exceeded the definition of a "place" for many of us; it is a "being" which captures our memories, our fascination and our delight.

This book is a story about a young man coming of age. Yet at the same time of being immersed in his own self-discovery he is being set in the middle of a revolutionary vision; the creation of an empire. His job enabled him to meet people from all walks of life and from all over the world. His awakening was further enhanced by the assorted people he met along the way that took him under their wing and help guide him into adulthood.

I met, or should I say, "found" Bob on a Disney themed site called "Jan's World." I was on the message boards and noticed someone was looking for Judy Marsh, the original Slue Foot Sue at the Golden Horseshoe Theatre. I contacted the person who posted the inquiry and very cautiously accessed their intentions. After having one conversation with Bob, it was clear to me that this man had loved Judy Marsh all his life. We shared this in common, as Judy Marsh was my mother.

Bob flew out the following Thanksgiving. At the time, my mother had suffered a debilitating stroke which had left her partially paralyzed and unable to speak. All I can say is that when their eyes met each other's gaze, there was no need for words. True love knows no time or disability. How privileged I was to see this relationship come full circle.

Sadly, my mother passed in 2008, yet her memory lives strong. In the book, I can see her so clearly. The woman that Bob describes in the book; beautiful, sensuous and kind was the woman I knew and still love.

She didn't speak often of her time as Slue Foot Sue and although she went on to a successful career as a singer, model, talent scout and even made a couple of movies; I think she regretted that her time at Disney was so short lived. When we went to Disneyland as children, she would point at the marquee and say, "See that line drawing of Slue Foot Sue, that is me!" One of her opening songs at the Golden Horseshoe was "Won't You Come Home Bill Bailey" and she would often erupt in that song with glee at home.

So, delight in your read. Immerse yourself in a time where life seemed more simple and transparent. Enjoy the magic Walt created and Bob and my mother were a part of. Remind yourself of the childlike imagination that Disney evoked and resides in each of us forever.

Preface
By David Koenig

According to Official Disney Company History, Disneyland launched its Tour Guide program in the fall of 1958, when the park was 26 months old. Seven cast members from various divisions were reassigned to staff the new operation.

Starting on September 17, 1958, guests could purchase a three-hour guided tour of the park for $3.25 per person, which included a strip of five tickets. Following their guide, guests would begin with a trip down Main Street on the double-decker Omnibus, head left to the Jungle Cruise, then circle the park clockwise, sampling one attraction in each land. Tours would end in front of Sleeping Beauty Castle, where the host or hostess would give each attendee a ticket to ride another attraction on their own and a Disneyland Souvenir Guide (a 25-cent value!).

For years, I believed that was the day Disneyland gave its first tours and that those seven staffers were the park's first tour guides. I believed that until I met Bob D'Arcy. As the park's 1955 employee directory confirms, Bob truly was Disneyland's first tour guide—although at the time he was referred to as a "host" or "Guest Relations assistant." He started giving tours in the spring of 1955, escorting VIP's through the construction site. Once the park opened, Bob became the park's first—and for several months only—guide, accompanying dignitaries, celebrities and Disney Studio representatives who required special access or privacy, as well as large groups that needed a little help keeping their parties organized. Unlike those "first tours" introduced 26 months later, Bob's services weren't advertised to or designed for regular visitors to the park.

So now for the first time in over 60 years, join Disneyland's original guide on a Walk in the Park.

Introduction

Walt Disney was so down to earth that he made me feel like he was my uncle. I never addressed him as uncle, always as "Walt." He wanted everyone to call him Walt, not Mr. Disney. I heard that one employee, who had a hard time accepting this, had been fired for continuing to call him Mr. Disney.

Walt really like kids, as this true story will confirm: Two girls, who were about 10 or 11 years old and lived near the park, would regularly climb the fence and sneak into the park. Late one afternoon as they were climbing back over the fence to go home, a security guard caught them and took them to the security office. One of the girls was really crying. As Walt walked by, he stopped to see what was going on. The girl who was not crying said they did not want to go to jail and asked the officers not to tell their parents. Walt gave them a little hug, walked them to the front gate, and told them they would not go to jail, but they must not do this again. He explained that he was concerned that they could be seriously hurt climbing the fence. He then gave them a big smile and sent them home. They could not believe that Walt would be so understanding and so kind to them.

Nevertheless, that was what Walt was all about. He could relate to the most intelligent men as well as a couple of kids in an emotionally stressful situation.

I was a very fortunate young man at the age of 22 when I first met him and began to be a part of his magnificent creation. Being a creative person myself and because of my job in the early days when Disneyland was "mud and cement," I had the privilege of experiencing the "Eighth Wonder of the World" (as I called it) become a reality.

This book is a tribute to Walt and my dear father, for without them I would have never had experienced this great part of my life.

I also dedicate some of this book to the great artists and art directors of the five "Lands," some of whom I worked with up close during the construction phase. I want to mention two very dedicated men who put the icing on this beautiful park—Jack and Bill Evans, of Evans & Reeves. They designed the landscaping, brought in every tree, and, with their fine staff, planted every plant. The landscaping was a very important part of Disneyland.

There was one real "uncle" I had by the name of Harry D'Arcy. Uncle Harry was one of the most loved men in the motion picture industry. I gave him a tour of the park and at the end of his tour, he said to me, "Bob, thanks for the fun tour, and if things should end here for you, look me up as I think you could make a career in the movie business." Uncle Harry, at this time, was Jack Webb's assistant director on the original *Dragnet* TV series. When I did leave Disneyland, Uncle Harry and his son (my cousin), Bill D'Arcy, also an assistant director, paved the way for my 30 years in television and feature films. And what a fun career it was.

In television, I worked steady as a stand-in and stunt double for Bob Denver on *Gilligan's Island*. During the same period, I worked on the great World War II drama *Combat*, where I learned the ropes of stunt work and occasionally doubled for Jack Hogan, who played Kirby. I became friends with its star, Vic Morrow, who loved music and we, along with the cast (who were just learning how to play their instruments), would meet at Vic's house to have "musicals."

Since *Gunsmoke*, the great western series, was filmed on the stage next to *Gilligan's Island*, I became acquainted with Ken Curtis, a.k.a. Festus. I also had the opportunity to work on the great western series, *Bonanza*. I became close friends with Dan Blocker, a.k.a. Hoss, who was a beautiful soul and a fun person to be around. In feature films, I worked primarily as a stand-in on the crew of David Walsh, a very fine cinematographer. I first joined David on *The Sunshine Boys* as a stand-in for George Burns. After that, we did many films including *Silver Streak, The Goodbye Girl, Only When I Laugh*, and *Private Benjamin*, where I met the lovely Goldie Hawn. Goldie became a special friend, as she helped me though a very dark period in my life. I will always love her. Thanks to David, a true loyal friend, I worked steady for about 12 years and met many great people in the film industry.

My story of Disneyland was to be in my autobiography that my dear daughter, Erin, had been after me to write for many, many years. She is a real history buff and wanted the history of our family to be well documented. My son, Eric, my partner in "the fun of life," also urged me to take on this project.

Perhaps one day I will write out the rest of my autobiography, but my Disneyland story seems an appropriate place to start.

I can't believe it has been 65 years since I walked the dirt roads of this soon-to-be-beautiful park, that the whole world was waiting to see and visit.

It was the greatest experience of my life to see all this beauty come to life on Opening Day.

So, to Walt, Dad, Mom, my children, and many friends...

Welcome to my Magic Kingdom!

1

November of 1954 was the beginning of the last winter I would have to spend in Anchorage, Alaska, as a member of the 43rd Army band. My tour of duty was to be over in January, and I looked forward to returning home and becoming a civilian once again.

My father, in one of his great letters to me, told of being selected out of about 100 men to be on the staff of Walt Disney as a food and restaurant consultant in the planning and development of Disneyland. Dad was in the restaurant business most of his life, mainly in management. He also founded the Drive-In and Restaurant Owners' Association of Southern California.

He told me of the high creative energy he was experiencing with Walt, and the many artists and art directors of Main Street, Adventureland, Frontierland, Fantasyland and Tomorrowland.

This was the first time I had ever heard the name Disneyland. I was so happy for Dad and now was eager to get home to see what was going on.

Being a lover of Disney's cartoons and especially the first feature animated movie, *Snow White and the Seven Dwarfs*, which I saw when I was six years old, I was excited about this new venture of Dad's. Little did I know what a great adventure it was going to be for me as well.

After I was finally discharged from the Army, I made my way back to the San Fernando Valley. Happy to be home, after all the hugs, I saw Dad's right foot, which had a huge bandage covering it all the way up to his shin. Due to Dad's poor health most of his life, a sore had developed on his foot. The doctor treating it botched the job and gangrene was forming. Walt was alarmed and sent him to his doctor, Danny Fortman, at St. Joseph's Hospital, right across from the Disney Studios. Dr. Fortman was the head surgeon for the Los Angeles Rams football team. Thank God, he saved Dad's foot. In that condition, since Mother did not drive and my brothers, Ron and Jim, were too young and still in school, I had to drive Dad everywhere.

The first drive was the following morning to Disney Studios. Leaving the parking lot and entering the studio, I was mesmerized. The vibrations were exciting, all the streets and buildings were named after all Walt's creations: Mickey Drive, Dopey Drive, Minnie Avenue, and, of course, the Mickey Mouse Theater.

Dad's office was in the huge animation building. It was a bright, wide-spaced room. Upon entering, the first thing I saw was a large detailed model of Main Street, complete with a flagpole. Being a model builder as a kid (I still like to build them now), I was so fascinated at the very entrance to the park. After walking around the model, Dad took me to his office where he showed me all the huge prints of the overall plot plan of the park, plus all the different Lands, which were all beautiful renderings by Walt's greatest artists.

Dad explained to me his part in this great creation. His part was to place the main restaurants, snack stands, and smaller restaurants, themed to each of the various Lands. Working with all the art directors, he had to placed them near the "guest flow" of traffic, without them getting in the way.

This was no easy task, considering they also had to comply with strict health and sanitary codes. For example, with the larger restaurants, you had to include an area called the "bull pen" for all the trash bins and storage supplies. The bull pens had to blend with the architecture of each specific Land and had to be included even in the smaller snack stands. The art directors had to cleverly design the pens so they would not be noticeable. In that regard, Dad continually worked closely with the sanitation department in Anaheim.

Dad was also involved in writing the leases that the original merchants and smaller business investors had to sign to be a part of Disneyland.

After spending the morning with Dad in his office, we broke for lunch. Heading for the commissary, we walked past the other large buildings with their manicured lawns and flowerbeds. As we neared the commissary, we noticed some employees were throwing around a football. Others were playing catch with a baseball. Three or four ping-pong tables were also in use. The atmosphere was very relaxed.

I thought, "What a great place to work at." Above the commissary, was the executive Green Room, a private dining room for the top brass; however, many a lunchtime Walt would join the line of employees in the commissary and chat with them. When someone further up the line would offer Walt their space, he would reply, "Thank you, but your time is just as valuable as mine, I'll wait my turn."

After lunch, as we took a different route back to the office, I asked Dad how his foot was feeling. He said if he walked slowly, it was OK. We walked by the Mickey Mouse Theater and passed a smaller building where the sounds of some great Dixieland jazz could be heard. I asked, "What's going on there?" Dad answered, "The Firehouse Five Plus Two is rehearsing." They were a group of Disney artists who were also talented musicians, and would get together at lunch and after work to play and prepare to make their first album on the Disney-owned Good Time Jazz label. There was a small group of employees standing around the open doors of this building enjoying the musical treat before returning to work. The banjo player in the group was a most interesting looking man, and I commented on him. Dad said, "That's Harper Goff. He's the art director of Adventureland." That is what really fascinated me about the studio—it was filled with so many multi-talented people.

Back at the office, Dad took me around the many rooms filled with artists and I met the various art directors. In addition to Harper Goff, I met Bill Martin, the art director of Fantasyland; Wade Rubottom, the art director of Main Street; George Patrick, the art director of Frontierland; and Gabe Scognamillio, the art director of Tomorrowland. At each art director's office, Dad would be asked his advice about a particular scenario, so the afternoon was a combined tour for me as well as a working one for Dad.

As an art lover and collector, of particular interest to me were the many sketches and renderings each department displayed across their expansive walls. Each room was an immense art gallery. Some were in color, some black and white, and all of them interesting.

The next day, I again drove Dad to the studio and hung out with him for part of the morning. I was so anxious to see more of the studio and asked Dad if it would be all right to take off on my own and tour the complex. He said, "Sure, if anyone asks about you, just tell them who you are and that you are taking care of your father."

I left the office and headed toward the back area of the studio to a very large building. As I approached the entrance, I heard hammering, buzz saws, and other construction-related sounds. I was neared the huge open door to the mill, which was a gigantic hall where many projects were being created and assembled. I stood at the door and wanted to go in, but I felt that I might be intruding, so I just looked in as far as I could. The first thing I saw was a life-sized model of a crocodile being pushed back and forth along a track by two craftsmen. The "croc" was tan in color and not yet fully made up to look like the real thing. After he was completely finished, he would go on another track in Adventureland to be shot at by the boat captains as a part of the Jungle River ride.

Looking to the right, I saw one of the first Dumbo bodies being molded in fiberglass. In another area, I saw the making of a Zulu warrior sans spear. I stood transfixed for about a half hour, before ultimately continuing on towards the back lot.

The back lot is the name studios call their exterior sets for filming movies. The first set I saw was a midwestern town, complete with storefronts, streets, sidewalks, curbs, lampposts and a chapel with a yard, enclosed by a picket fence. A small park was off to one side surrounded by pretty trees, flowerbeds and a couple of benches. I sat down on one and felt the magic of Hollywood. I had just left a working mill and 50 yards away, I was in the Midwest. When I got up and walked through the park, I was suddenly in an old western town—shabby old buildings, a livery stable, a big old barn, water troughs for the horses to drink from, old wooden sidewalks with gas lampposts, and some scattered chairs and benches. This old frontier town really took me back to my younger days, when I loved going to the Saturday matinee to see the old B western movies.

I left the Old West and just around the corner was a modern American city, circa 1954. It was a small one, though, with a block of two-story buildings, a bank, post office, and theater.

It was nearing lunchtime, so I headed back to Dad's office. Upon entering, there was the man himself, Walt Disney. I stopped at the door, not wanting to intrude on their conversation, and Dad said, "Come in, Son, and meet Walt." For some reason, I was not overwhelmed with a feeling of awe; I felt very much at ease. Walt said, "Nice to meet you, Bob," and excused himself as their meeting had just ended. After he left, I had a great warm feeling of meeting one of the most famous, creative men in the world. Never in my wildest dreams did I anticipate we would have many more encounters of a personal nature in the future.

Over the next few days, I would drop Dad off at the studio, return home to visit with Mother and my brothers, and get back into the groove of civilian life. In the afternoon, I would pick up Dad, and then it was home for dinner. Dad would then proceed to recap what had developed that day at the studio. On Tuesday nights, we would watch Walt's hour-long show on ABC. A special segment on the show was Walt's ten minute "Progress Report of the Construction of Disneyland." In watching these reports, I felt eager to be there and see for myself this great wonder develop.

About a week later, I would get to see that wish come true.

2

Dad was the first one of the "founding group"—as members of the studio team called themselves—to be relocated to the "site," as the park was then known. He was sent down to work with the project engineer, Lou Roth, and the construction head, George Mills, in regards to the bull pens as well as to establish relations with the health and sanitation departments, and other members of the Anaheim city government.

At this time, the Santa Ana Freeway had not yet been completed. The round-trip drive from Los Angeles to Anaheim took about three hours—entirely too much traveling time to drive on a daily basis. So I finally said, "Dad, see if you can get me some kind of a job so we can work together and make one trip."

I do not know with whom Dad talked to about my proposal, but I was hired to work in the project engineer's office. I was to receive the daily shipment of blueprints from the studio and distribute them—one set to George Mills, the head of construction; one set to Evans and Reeves, the landscaping firm that did the principal landscaping of all of Disneyland; and the master set for our office.

Lou Roth was a nice man as well as a very busy man. One day he told me, "After the plans come in, usually in the afternoon, I want you to take Walt's Jeep and get familiar with every Land." He wanted me to know where every shop, ride and building was going to be located. He continued, "Many investors and future lessees are starting to come to the site. They want to see the location where their businesses will be situated, and I am getting too busy to do that anymore. From now on, you will handle that task for me." That was the beginning for Disneyland's first host.

Working with the blueprints, I learned where most of the smaller businesses, mainly shops, were located. The larger ones—Swift and Company, Pepsi-Cola, Coca-Cola, TWA, Wurlitzer Organs, and Bank of America—were easy to spot. TWA would have the huge rocket in Tomorrowland, but at that time it was only a marked-off area. Its landmark would arrive and be put into place about a month before ABC's premiere television broadcast.

At 4:30 every afternoon, all worked stopped on the site. All the carpenters, laborers and electricians left and the park became suddenly silent. That is when I would climb into Walt's black Jeep and have the park all to myself. With no one left on property except for Mr. Roth and my Dad tucked away in his office, I felt like the king of a growing country. While I was in the Army in Alaska, I had purchased a Kodak Signet 35mm camera and took only slide pictures instead of prints. So on my journeys through the park, I captured most everything from its infancy to its complete form on Opening Day. These afternoons were my favorite times. It was thrilling to have an opportunity most photographers—not to mention the millions of future guests—would die for.

MY FIRST Disneyland ID card, issued by park executive Fred Schumacher.

When I would get my slides back from the developer, it was truly exciting to see how beautifully they turned out. Speaking of photographs, Walt had three very high towers equipped with stop-motion cameras. These cameras shot an overall area picture every 29 seconds. They were for Walt's study of the progress being made. He also used them for the construction progress reports on his TV weekly show. Showing the film in 29-second intervals made them look like old silent movies that showed the progress of the building of the park.

During one of my late afternoon tours, I came upon a man with a movie camera filming Main Street. This is the first time I saw anyone in the park at that hour. I introduced myself, and he asked me what my job was. I told him my job and duties, then added, "May I ask you the same question?" He laughed and said, "My name is Stuart Jewell. I'm one of Walt's True Life Adventures cinematographers assigned to photograph the building of the park." We became fast friends, and from time to time Stuart would ask me if I could help him on special projects. I would drive his station wagon very slowly while he lay on the hood so he could shoot some moving motion on film. I was delighted and performed as his driver many times. At this time, I still did not know the purpose of the towers. One afternoon, Stuart met me in the Jeep and said, "Can you spare some time?" I nodded, and he said, "Follow me."

We headed past Frontierland, along the service road to the edge of the park, and stopped at the gigantic warehouse where Walt had stored many components to the different attractions in the park. Stuart was doing a story on the many machines that would be placed in the Penny Arcade on Main Street. After choosing one, he said, "I'm going to need your help in focusing. I'll show you how."

Several minutes later, I was ready and Stuart took the back panel off the machine to reveal the many parts, chains, disks and various other elements that made it work. He filmed the overall front. Then we moved in slowly and panned around to the side, and continued slowly to the exposed back, then moved in close to reveal all the workings. This all took about 20 minutes. It was a kick not only to do it, but also to see it shown on the weekly ABC show.

I left Stuart and headed back, stopping at different structures to take more pictures, then parked the Jeep and walked over to Dad's office. He was still working and said it would be about a half-hour or so before we went home. I said I would be waiting in the car. I was seated listening to one of my favorite jazz stations on the radio. Joe Adams, the same man who would later manage the great Ray Charles, hosted the show. I had the volume down low, fortunately. I say this because suddenly I heard some loud, strong language. Walt and C.V. Wood were in an intense argument. C.V. Wood was Disneyland's first general manager. Walt growled, "This happens to be Disneyland, not C.V. Woodland," followed by more strong language. C.V. was a young man from Oklahoma who was responsible for negotiating with some reluctant landowners to sell to Disney. He had come to Disneyland via the Stanford Research Institute, the firm hired by Disney to find the location for Disneyland.

Walt and C.V. were standing on the steps of the first administration building, an old house that used to belong to one of the families that once owned the property. The two of them were about 30 feet behind me and I slowly sunk as low as I could in the seat of my car and froze! I thought, "If Walt were to see me now, knowing I innocently overheard this entire conversation, what would happen to me since he's so very mad and upset?" As luck would have it, my car was parked four or five stalls away and when they were finished, they went their separate ways. Fortunately, neither one saw me.

When Dad returned to the car, I told him what had just happened. He said, "You were lucky, Laddie. I don't know how Walt would have reacted, but it would have put us both in an awkward situation."

On the way home, Dad told me some other things about Walt. "Just do a good job and don't try to get too close to him," Dad advised. "Remember that he cannot stand to be addressed as 'Mr. Disney' and, above all, he hates snitches."

3

I looked forward to returning to the park every morning. It was a constant delight watching everything developing step by step—the landscaping slowly forming, huge trees arriving in monstrous wood planters, the constant noise of hammers and wood saws, water trucks watering down the dusty dirt streets, cement trucks unloading into founding forms. There were also the ever-present sounds of the tractors moving earth to form the "berm," which would separate Disneyland from the outside world. Many mornings, if Lou did not need me, I would just walk the whole park and see everything "close up." I would walk into the Golden Horseshoe Saloon and try to visualize how it was going to look when completed. I would then look at the track the Mark Twain riverboat would ride on and watch the hull of the mighty paddlewheeler in dry dock, where later the Mike Fink Keel Boats would find their home. I would then walk through the Painted Desert, seeing it taking shape. The creative vibrations of all this was something I will never forget. It was truly magical.

Walt was always thinking ahead, and he could change his mind on a moment's notice. One afternoon, just before quitting time, the large gazebo, which I had seen being constructed in the mill, was brought out by a large crane. It slowly made its way to the center of Town Square, just inside the entrance to the park where the flagpole now stands. It was placed on the designated spot and the crane gradually lowered it into place. It looked great, blending with the architecture of the Main Street buildings, which were nearing completion. It was almost like a mini-ceremony. I watched along with Lou Roth, George Mills, and others from the construction crew; we were delighted to see this fine structure finally in place.

MAIN STREET Train Station was the subject of one of the first construction shots I took in the spring of 1955.

The next morning, on my way to Lou's office, I looked at an empty Town Square. I asked Lou what had happened. He explained that Walt had come out after everyone but Lou had gone home and realized he had made a wrong decision in placing the gazebo there. The gazebo had originally been intended for afternoon concerts with the Disneyland Band, but he realized, with the guests sitting and standing around listening to the concert, it would create a huge, unwanted bottleneck. I asked what he had done with it. Lou said, "Take a walk down by the castle and you will see it." I did, and there it was, seated in the middle of an area between the large fence of Frontierland and the moat and drawbridge entrance to Fantasyland. Looking forward to the first Christmas at Disneyland, the area was appropriately named the Christmas Bowl.

THE EMPORIUM on Main Street begins to take shape.

One afternoon, Lou informed me that a woman, accompanied by her mother and father, was due to arrive soon and that I should get the Jeep. I was to meet them at the entrance and give them a tour. He said the woman was from the studio and that she was not an investor. I met the group and assisted the older mother and father into the Jeep. The woman got in the front seat next to me. I paused and explained the entrance and the five-eighths scale railroad station. In fact, most of Disneyland is built in five-eighths scale.

As I was about halfway down Main Street, this woman kept interjecting comments such as, "And here, Dad, will be a turn-of-the-century Penny Arcade and here will be the Emporium." When she finished her talk, I said, "Usually, when I take someone through the park, they have very little knowledge of Disneyland. You seem

SWIFT'S RED WAGON INN, with its red-shingled roof, was built off the Hub at the end of Main Street and would be Disneyland's fanciest restaurant.

to know as much as I do!" She replied, "I should know a lot about this park—I have been Roy Disney's personal secretary since 1928." I was quite taken back by this and said, "Would you like for me to just drive, and you can tell your folks the whole story?" She said, "Oh no, you are doing a splendid job. By the way, my name is Madeline Wheeler." I introduced myself and we continued on.

After the tour, I walked them to the front gate and Madeline asked me what my ambition in life was. I told her I had put in an application to study music at the University of Mexico under the G.I. Bill, because of the money ratio. I could live quite well and study without the financial burden, but at the same time, their quota was filled and I was waiting my turn. She thanked me for the tour and said if there was any way she could help me, I should just

COCA-COLA REFRESHMENT CENTER was placed at the northwestern-most corner of Main Street.

PLACING TREES in Frontierland.

THE MAKINGS of Disneyland's New Orleans Street, with Casa de Fritos (center) and Aunt Jemima's Pancake House (far right).

MARK TWAIN is coming together.

call her at the Studio. On the way home that day, I mentioned to Dad about my encounter with Madeline. He gave me a startled look and said, "You just met the most powerful woman in the organization." Later in my life, I did call her and she was a great help to me.

Each day, as construction was nearing completion, the pace around the park was becoming very hectic. More volumes of blueprints had to be filed and additional tours given to investors. Speaking of investors, one day during this time, I piled into the Jeep three guys from ABC Paramount Corporation. After they saw the different areas of the park, they wanted a tour of the route the Mark Twain would take down the Rivers of America. We took off and ended up at the dock area where guests would board the ride. The dock was not yet built and all that existed was an eight-foot berm

GOLDEN HORSEHOE is coming along.

of earth, at a steep angle. I paused, put the Jeep in four-wheel drive, and started up the slope. I noticed the wide eyes and white knuckles of the man next to me. It also suddenly occurred to me that I had never done this before. My eyes similarly widened as I found myself in this most precarious situation. Fortunately, I continued as if this was standard procedure and we made it to the top in front of the Golden Horseshoe. I said, "Would you like to see more of the park?" The look on their faces answered my question, "No thank you, young man. We would like to return to the front gate."

As the park was taking shape, two structures in particular were my favorites and, I think, the most interesting: Sleeping Beauty Castle and the Plaza Pavilion. The Pavilion was a two-faced building; one side, facing Main Street, had a turn-of-the-century facade and the other side, facing Adventureland, had a Polynesian

PLAZA PAVILION would have a Victorian motif when viewed from Main Street (top) and a Polynesian look when viewed from Adventureland (below).

SLEEPING BEAUTY CASTLE receives its spectacular face.

facade. I was fascinated to see each side slowly blend into its respective Land without the differences between the two styles being so noticeable when the building was finally completed. When you're in Adventureland, you never realize that the other side is completely different. The Pavilion was a large cafeteria-style restaurant and the only building in the park that had two art directors: Wade Rubottom of Main Street and Harper Goff of Adventureland.

Sleeping Beauty Castle was patterned after an old castle in Bavaria. Watching it grow gradually was quite an experience. Who gets to see something like this being created? First, it was wood, built like any other building. Then plaster molds of large archways and turrets were sculpted and put in place. Three-quarters of the castle was made to look like old stone facing, all done using movie

BACK VIEW of the castle construction, taken from the Fantasyland courtyard.

studio techniques. The upper quarter was done in a smooth plaster look. Some of the top turret covers were built in the mill and placed on top with a large crane. It was the detail of the finished structure that was so amazing. If you took a full shot of it with a camera and showed it to someone who did not know anything about Disneyland, then told them you took the picture during a visit to Europe, they would never know its true location.

One particularly busy day, Lou told me that Harper Goff wanted me to see him in Adventureland. When I got there, Harper was at the dock. He said, "Bob, we are going to mark the support posts for the track that the boats will ride on." There on the riverbed was Walt's Jeep with a simulated boat made of two-by-fours attached on the head of the Jeep. The fake boat had the exact dimensions, in

CASTLE HAS been plastered and is ready for its paint job.

width, of the real boat. Harper instructed me to drive the Jeep
slowly down the middle of the riverbed and when he said, "Hold
it!" I was to stop. At this point, he would get out and drive a stake
where the support post would be placed. We were about halfway
down the riverbed when I thought, "What a great experience. Here
I am with the art director, actually laying the track for the Jungle
Cruise."

As Opening Day grew closer, things really started happening fast.
The Mark Twain was completed and set on its track. Water started
to fill the Rivers of America. The Mad Tea Party had its spinning
teacups in place and was nearing "test time." The Autopia was laid
out and cars were beginning to take test runs around the course.
Peter Pan Flight, Mr. Toad's Wild Ride, and the Snow White dark

ADVENTURELAND ENTRANCE with bridge in its primitive stages.

ride were getting ready to test, as well. Casey Jr. Circus Train's track was completed; the Chicken of the Sea pirate ship was almost ready. There was so much going on that I had a tough time keeping track of everything.

During all this heavy activity, one of the first of many parties was held after work, this one at an old two-story house on the site where the Disneyland Hotel was under construction. The house was to be razed the next day. At this time, as some of the department heads and other executives were settling into their new offices, somebody got a bright idea to have a "destruction party." Some of the group set up a bar on a makeshift counter and stocked it with every kind of booze, including a big tub of ice filled with beer and wine. We started by making a series of toasts. "Here's to Disneyland!" And

JUNGLE RIVER boathouse was originally built with a second-story outlook/break room for the skippers.

everyone drank. "Here's to the Disneyland Hotel!" And everyone drank. "Here's to Walt!" And so on.

Then the fun began. After one toast, somebody thew his glass through a window. Well, naturally everybody followed suit, including throwing beer bottles. When the alcohol started to kick in, the party really got crazy. At one point, I looked over to the stairway to see three guys coming down with a bathtub, followed by a sink with some plumbing attached. Doorknobs were being thrown at walls, making gaping holes. It really became a comedy as everybody tried to outdo each other, laughing wildly all the way. When it all ended, there was not one window left intact and all the walls were destroyed. Even the kitchen sink wound up in the backyard. This was just the first of many parties at the park, but this

CAMBODIAN RUINS were one of the first show scenes crafted for the Jungle Cruise.

was the one and only destruction party.

Back at the park, all those blueprints I had filed during the last six months were becoming a reality. The painters were starting to show color on all the buildings. The Police Station, City Hall, and the Fire Station (where Walt's private second-story apartment was located) were nearing completion. Bank of America was becoming operational. Wurlitzer was moving in organs as well as one of the world's first electronic pianos.

At about this time, the TWA rocket was being installed in Tomorrowland. The carousel arrived in Fantasyland, as well as the Dumbo ride. The Golden Horseshoe interior decoration was also in full swing. All the restaurants were being equipped with ovens, grills, soda fountains, and seating. On the perimeter, behind

ADVENTURELAND BAZAAR was the land's primary retail center.

Frontierland and Fantasyland, were the stables where all the livestock was being quartered. The big Clydesdale horses would pull the streetcars down Main Street while others would pull the surreys. There were even special five-eighths scale horses to carry passengers on the five-eighths scale stagecoaches through the Painted Desert. This was all happening under the training and watchful eye of Owen Pope, who managed the stables.

The landscaping was looking more beautiful every day. Most of the trees were planted, along with a dazzling display of colorful flowerbeds framing the Main Street Railroad Station, with a floral Mickey Mouse in the middle. The beautiful, manicured flowerbeds that were planted throughout the park were a tribute to the great creative work of Jack and Bill Evans, two great guys with a very fine

CHICKEN OF THE SEA Pirate Ship was a rush job to finish on time.

staff.

The streetcar tracks were being installed on Main Street and asphalt would soon follow. All the windows on the second stories along Main Street were being painted with names of the small businesses, such as lawyers' and dentists' offices, which were made to look as if you could just walk upstairs and do business. Real gas street lamps were in and being tested.

The end was near and the great beginning was just a couple of weeks away. I had mixed feelings about this. Being a creative person, I really enjoyed the construction phase, seeing everything develop into the beauty of it all. It gave me such a special feeling, as I had never experienced before in my life.

As the big day approached, I walked into Frontierland to see the one area I found so fascinating. The stagecoach stop where guests would board the ride through the Painted Desert, a mining town, was created with the illusion that it went deeper into the mountain than it actually did. In reality, it was only about three layers of buildings built in perspective—large buildings in front, smaller ones behind that, and even smaller ones behind them—more Disney magic that was most effective. The stagecoaches were in five-eighths scale and were truly beautiful in every detail. I have often wondered what happened to them when the ride was later discontinued.

The Golden Horseshoe, when first completed, was also stunning. All the flocked wallpaper, the stage with the polished wood floors, the opera boxes on each side, VIP and special guest seating, the orchestra pit, the long bar where one would step up and have a frothy Pepsi, were all done in the style true to the period, complete with sparkling chandeliers.

The Mark Twain looked magnificent at the dock. As I went aboard and walked the main deck, I noticed how authentic it looked. Climbing to the second deck, I noted the ceiling's bright light illuminated the many posts that supported the top deck with their upper support brackets that looked like lace, and formed an arch effect look that truly defined the old riverboats. On the third deck was the pilot's cabin. As I stood behind the large wheel that

WORKMEN PUT the finishing touches on the Main Street Cinema.

actually turned, it gave the illusion that you were actually steering the ship. Only VIP's and special guests were allowed in the pilot's cabin. To the side of the wheel was a drawer stocked with official "Mark Twain Pilot's Licenses" that were given to those special guests. The paddlewheel at the rear of the ship was an actual steam-driven engine that powered the Mark Twain, again in smaller scale. As always, Walt insisted that every detail be authentic.

I left the Mark Twain and headed for New Orleans Street. It looked very much like an actual section of the French Quarter. Aunt Jemima's Pancake House was close to opening for breakfast. The buildings between Aunt Jemima's and the Golden Horseshoe had an upper story that housed the dressing rooms for the cast of the show. Looking at the river from the end of New Orleans Street, I

THE ORIGINAL Frontierland Train Station and the Disneyland Railroad's "cattle cars."

could see a gazebo where guests could sit and watch the Mark Twain as it passed down the river. At the very end of the New Orleans section, near the tracks of the Disneyland Railroad, was a smaller railroad station with a mock-up water tower. I left New Orleans and walked to the Painted Desert. It was looking more authentic with the natural arch bridge and the balancing rock. All the landscaping was in and the cacti had been planted. The stagecoaches with their four five-eighths scale horses were making test runs.

During this time, the hectic pace continued. The Golden Horseshoe show was in full rehearsal. The Pendleton Woolen Mills store was being stocked with its famous shirts, blankets and other fine goods by Bill Carpenter, the store's first manager. "Lucky" was Frontierland's first sheriff and he was undergoing training on how to "tame this wild town" and how to keep the "evil Black Bart" from causing trouble. It was during this time that Disneyland's first employees were hired and trained for their jobs.

Maybe because I am a musician, I am conscious of the sounds around me. I stood for a moment and reflected on the past and present multitude of sounds: the early construction noise, the finishing phase, and now the sounds of completing the project and the feelings of urgency to meet the deadline of July 17 for the TV premiere that would present Disneyland to the world.

I walked through the gates of Frontierland and stood at the Hub, as we called the large circular Plaza. It was from this "wheel" area at the end of Main Street that all the Lands spun off. What a sight it was for me: the Victorian side of the Pavilion, Adventureland's tiki entrance, Frontierland's old fort fence and tower, and the Christmas Bowl area, now stocked with rows of benches for guests to sit and enjoy the upcoming holiday shows. The stunning Sleeping Beauty Castle was all decked out with small flags on its spires, set behind beautiful lawns, flowerbeds and a moat now filled with water in addition to black and white swans swimming about. What a magnificent picture and a signature statement of the park, as well as an exciting entrance to Fantasyland. Looking towards the entrance to Tomorrowland there was a huge pillar structure with color patterns at the top that housed a clock that gave the time everywhere in the world.

Next to Tomorrowland was Swift and Company's Red Wagon Inn. At this time, the Red Wagon was the largest restaurant in the park. When you walked in, you would see a reception desk and waiting area, then off to each side were long wings that were the primary seating for guests. As you entered, the right wing, tucked behind the wall, was Walt's private dining room. You would enter through a sliding door that was all but invisible. It was a very elegant room with flocked wallpaper, elegant drapery treatments, beautiful furnishings, and table settings all reflecting the turn-of-the-century decor.

Tomorrowland was the only Land that seemed empty to me. The entrance, apart from the Clock of the World, consisted of two large buildings, mainly leased by big corporations, such as Kaiser Aluminum and Monsanto Chemicals. They featured scientific exhibits that were not particularly exciting, as far as I was concerned. A walk-through exhibit recreating the Nautilus submarine from the movie *20,000 Leagues Under the Sea* was still under construction.

The only interesting exhibit was in a large room where a 360-degree screen was erected that featured a motion picture of a trip through Los Angeles in full color. You would stand in the middle of the room and see the full trip anywhere you looked. This unique attraction was named the Circarama. In addition, the Autopia was not too exciting in its initial concept. It experienced frequent breakdowns with the cars. The TWA Rocket to the Moon ride was a different type of ride. As you entered a large circular room, there was seating around a large circle screen. At the bottom of the screen, you would see the blast off and the continued journey to the moon. The sound effects were rather primitive but still somewhat effective. The most impressive part of the ride was the entrance: a very tall rocket set on a tripod. All of Tomorrowland appeared to have a bland look about it, unlike the other Lands, which were rich in detail, color and vegetation.

As I walked through the castle into Fantasyland, Merlin's Magic Shop was being stocked with its mystery merchandise. The first thing you would notice was is the carousel, with its bright colors and finely detailed carved horses and the musical sound of a calliope.

Some of the new employees and a few staff members were sampling test runs on the dark rides (Snow White, Mr. Toad's Wild Ride, and Peter Pan). I found the Snow White ride to be the most entertaining. At one turn, you encountered the wicked witch giving you her weird look as she held the poison apple and said, "Have an apple, dearie." For some reason that little piece of dialog really caught our attention as we took the first test rides and soon everyone was saying, "Have an apple, dearie." The Mickey Mouse Theater was showing cartoons on the new screen. Casey Jr. Circus Train was still working out some bugs, but looked like it would be ready in time.

Some of the main attractions of Fantasyland were not yet completed. The interior of Sleeping Beauty Castle was still in the framework stages; there were only crude stairways to a few platforms leading to the very top. I had access to the keys that locked the

TWA ROCKET TO THE MOON was one of the few completed elements of Tomorrow-land by Opening Day.

doors, one door at each side at the rear of the castle, and at times, I would climb to the top platform and view all of the action taking place in the park. It was a great vantage point to see most of the Lands.

Moving over to Adventureland, the entrance really set the mood and visually put you into a true jungle atmosphere. The first building to the right was the Adventureland Bazaar, a large shop being set up with exotic gifts, teas and other interesting merchandise. Part of the Bazaar was leased by Davey Lee. He and his family owned General Lee's, one of the finest restaurants in Los Angeles' Chinatown. Dad and Davey developed a beautiful relationship, and I became friends with him as well. He liked our whole family and gave us all an open invitation to have dinner at his fine restaurant and, many times, tickets to the L.A. Philharmonic Auditorium. We saw many of the top musicals from Broadway and Davey always picked up the tab.

The river was now full and the boats were making trial runs. The dock and boathouse looked so realistic, you could actually visualize being in a village somewhere along the Amazon River.

I climbed aboard for a ride and saw the vegetation in full bloom, the Cambodian temple, Blinky the giraffe, and one of those crocodiles I had seen earlier at the studio, now looking very real and menacing. The Zulu warriors with their spears and the hippos, one coming close to the boat with its mouth wide open, were other great effects. I thought back to when Harper and I had measured and staked out the track I was now riding on, knowing that most of the guests were not aware it even existed. The skippers looked great in their wardrobe and their firing guns at the hippos, and crocodiles were a great finishing touch to the cruise.

A funny thing happened regarding the Zulu warriors. Work on the final landscaping required a night shift in the hectic race to complete the work in time for the TV premiere. An Asian gardener, starting his shift, was unaware of the warriors that had been placed in the jungle that day. They were in full costume, complete with spears, looking completely authentic. As the gardener finished up in the area where he had been working, he turned the corner and ran smack into the Zulu warriors. The gardener screamed, and the other workers turned to see him running out of the jungle, down the service road, out the front gate, and into the parking lot. Needless to say, he refused to work in that area again.

I was so pleased by the way Adventureland had evolved, as it was one of my favorite areas. I visited and photographed almost every day during the construction phase.

I walked through the Pavilion on to Main Street. There was constant activity, the asphalt was completed, and the streetcars were taking passengers around the flagpole down Main Street to the Hub and back again. The "clop, clop" sound of those mammoth horses took you back in time to when that was one of the primary modes of transportation. What made it seem even more realistic were the mounds of horse manure left to be scooped up. A little man named Trinidad performed this task. Dressed all in white, complete with a pith helmet, he became one of the most popular characters on Main Street.

Painting was still in the works in the interior of the shops as merchandise was arriving in boxes. From the Penny Arcade, you could hear the sounds from the old amusement machines. I rounded the corner where the Emporium was being stocked and stopped at the Fire Station. The old fire engine was in its stall, and above, Walt's private apartment was being decorated with antique furniture and priceless art pieces and paintings. Next to the Fire Station, the City Hall was now complete. Upon entering, a huge desk was to become the guest information center. A lovely woman by the name of Kaye Hooton ran it. She was perfectly cast; she possessed a fun personality, was pretty, most helpful, and we became great friends. Next to City Hall was the Police Station. At this time, I did not know that this would very soon become my office as Guest Relations assistant.

I walked up the stairs to the Disneyland Railroad Station and waited for the train to arrive. The train was Walt's personal favorite part of the park. He had been a railroad enthusiast since his

CITY HALL receptionist Kaye Hooton.

childhood. He had a much smaller railroad in the backyard of his Holmby Hills home. Although I never had the privilege to see it, I was told it was quite elaborate. I boarded the train, and for the first time, saw the park from a completely different perspective. I saw all the Lands from the rear, other than just from the front. The ride was smooth and very interesting.

4

Time was getting short now as the TV premiere on ABC was just over a week away. It was about this time that I received my assignment from the studio as Guest Relations assistant and moved into my office in the Police Station. I felt great to be finally getting my permanent job status, which also came with my own secretary. Her name was Barbara. She was a lovely young lady and if you should read this, Barbara, forgive me for not remembering your last name. All I remember is calling you by your first name, although I still remember your pretty face. The Police Station was unique in that it had its front door off Main Street and a rear door that opened to the service road. The rear location was at the end of Adventureland. About 25 feet down the road was an area where the mechanical workings of Blinky the giraffe were located. Blinky's long neck and head with his mouth chewing grass was all there was to him. He would swing around the service road, make a long swoop and would become visible to the guests taking the boat ride. All they could see was his long neck and mouth chewing grass. The boat captain's story would be something like, "And over there, folks, is old Blinky the giraffe, one of our favorites in the jungle."

I think I had the greatest office in the park. My colleagues, events planner Tommy Walker and PR specialist Cap Blackburn, were in City Hall. I was close to the front gate, so I had a short walk to meet the many people I would escort through the park.

My first official assignment from the Studio was to greet one of the most beautiful actresses of the Thirties and Forties, Miss Irene Dunne. Irene was to christen the Mark Twain during the TV premiere. Walt chose Irene mainly because her grandfather used to build riverboats near the turn of the century.

MY FIRST BUSINESS CARD, as the first host of Disneyland's new Guest Relations Department.

Walt wanted authenticity even to this degree. I met Irene at the main gate, and she was beautifully dressed in white with matching accessories. She had a wonderfully warm personality and was very friendly. As I walked her down Main Street, she asked me many questions about myself: how I became involved in Guest Relations and what had I done previously. She reminisced about the architecture of Main Street, which took her back to her childhood. We entered Frontierland, and she said, "What a grand sight. Everything seems so real. It reminds me of some of the westerns I have worked on." We walked past all the activity and reached the dock and the Mark Twain. Two cameras were setup at different angles. Her chair was placed nearby and the director introduced himself to us. Before he started to explain the scene, she asked me if I would be back to meet her when she was finished with the rehearsal. I told her that Walt had wanted me to stay with her at all times. She was delighted and began to rehearse. I sat in a chair nearby and thought, "Seven months ago, I was in the Army in frozen Alaska and, in that time since, I have lived Walt's fantasy and vision and have become a permanent part of his reality. How blessed can you get?" To top it off, I was escorting one of the most beautiful women in the world through it all. After the rehearsal, Irene said,

ONE OF THE FIRST trips by the Mark Twain across the Rivers of America, with Walt at the forefront of the action.

"Bob, I'm taking part in this grand venture, and I know very little about it. Could you take me around and explain what it is all about?" I said I would be most happy to do so. She put her arm in mine and off I walked with this most elegant woman, giving her the first assigned tour in my newly appointed position. I felt extremely proud, not to mention that we were the talk of the park. Ending the tour, I brought her to the Maxwell House Coffee House in Town Square to meet Dad, as she was one of his favorite actresses. He was overwhelmed, just one of the many times I would bring VIP celebrities and stars to meet the man I was so proud to call my

DISNEYLAND HOST ribbon made me instantly visible to my VIP's.

MY DAD, James D'Arcy, makes himself at home in his new base of operations, the Maxwell House Coffee House on Main Street.

father. I walked Irene to the front gate, she thanked me for the tour, gave me a nice hug, and said, "See you tomorrow."

By this time, Dad's work was finished working directly for Disneyland, since his main function had been in the construction phase. He then formed his own company called Food Services, Inc. That was a consulting firm to the various restaurants, guiding them on their initial set-up and operating methods. However, his real participation in the park was as the General Manager of the Maxwell House, an authentic reproduction of the original Maxwell House Coffee Shop and Restaurant in New Orleans.

Inside, past the reception desk, to the left, in a corner, was a large table with four chairs. This was where Dad sat most of the time and held court. By that, I mean, many of the employees got to know him and, as Dad was very intellectual, he would give them his advice on their specific problems.

One of my fondest memories of that time was the night before opening day. I went over to the Maxwell House to see how Dad was doing getting the restaurant ready for the opening. He said he was in good shape. He was seated at the corner table with Mother. We sipped a cup of coffee, and when we were through, Dad said, "Let's take a walk around the park." We strolled up Main Street, and when we reached the Hub, we stopped and observed all the last minute preparations taking place. The special lighting on the castle looked so beautiful, Frontierland's entrance and the world clock opening into Tomorrowland were dramatically lit as well. As we stood taking in all this wonder, Dad said, "Remember this night, Son. You are a part of one of the most spectacular attractions in the world."

We continued our walk, and I became so aware of my surroundings: so new, so sparkling, the smell of fresh paint and the sounds of the new rides, the horses pulling the trolleys and the surreys. We arrived at the Golden Horseshoe, one of Dad's favorite spots. It was a colorful sight, with the chandeliers ablaze, the stage with its footlights striking the backdrop. It soon became one of my very favorite places in the park, as well.

We returned to the Maxwell House and Dad made a final check to be sure everything was ready for the next big day. I will never forget that evening, how close we were, the three of us, and I fully realized how very blessed I was to be a part of Walt's dream and the son of a great father and mother.

The next day, July 17, Irene was not due until late afternoon to perform her part in the show. In the morning, when I arrived at my office, Ed Ettinger, the head of publicity, called and said, "Bob, I need your help. My staff is extremely busy and I need you to screen the invited guest list and not let anyone in who is not on that list." Part of my job was to assist publicity when they needed me, if I was not involved in a special tour. Well, that list Ed sent over was about as thick as *Gone with the Wind*. So there I was at 10:00 A.M. at the Main Gate, dressed in a white dinner jacket, black slacks, light blue shirt, and black tie. I only mention this because it was in the middle of July and I was roasting in the summer heat. Screening was no easy task as there must have been 1,000 or more uninvited people all wanting to get in. I was propositioned by a couple of pretty ladies, offered money, cigarettes, liquor and items I have long forgotten. I stood there for about three hours before I went through the list. I stopped by my office to see if anything new had come in. There was nothing except to meet Irene at 4:00 P.M. I went to Carnation's Ice Cream Parlor for lunch, then I walked to Fantasyland to see the TV broadcast crew and observe the organized confusion. The place was a beehive of activity. People were running everywhere. Camera cables were scattered around the Teacup ride. In fact, it seemed like cable was covering the entire Land. What a sight. I watched Art Linkletter rehearsing his part of the show. I always enjoyed his shows dealing with kids.

I headed back to the office and relaxed for a while. The entire park was so busy and it was beginning to wear me out. Irene arrived on time. I met her and we walked over to Frontierland, heading to the Mark Twain. She rehearsed once more then sat in her chair awaiting her cue. When that time arrived, she was terrific. When she was finished, she remarked that we had better leave as she had a party to attend early that evening. At the front gate, she thanked me again for my help, gave me another hug, entered her limousine, and was gone.

I went up to Frontierland to enjoy the action at the Golden Horseshoe. Cameras were set up to film the show. I walked in and who did I see standing at the bar but Dad, wearing a Stetson hat he had borrowed from the wardrobe department. He looked great and was having a grand time being part of the celebration. I watched the Golden Horseshoe Revue for the first of many times and found my eyes focused on Slue Foot Sue, the star of the show. Other stars in the cast were Irish tenor Don Novis, one of Walt's old friends, and Wally Boag, a wild comedian who made animals from balloons. Judy Marsh played Slue Foot Sue. She not only sang beautifully, but she was a gorgeous blonde with a lovely body and a very warm personality.

It was a great show and soon became one of the highlights of the park. Dad had brought Mother with him and I spotted her at a table. I sat with her until the end of the show when Dad joined us for a Pepsi. Mother was a very special lady. Dad was a victim of rheumatoid arthritis and she was continually trying to ease his pain, which took a lot of work, in addition to keeping house. By this time, my brother, Ron, my sister, Bobbie, and my youngest brother, Jim, all worked at the park. Dear Mother kept all of us in clean, pressed shirts and pants, including our costumes. Additionally, she was one of the best cooks around and always had a smile on her face. After the show, we went home, tired from a long and active day.

5

Back then, we considered Opening Day to actually be July 18—
the first day the park would be open to the public. It was finally
here, and what a day it was! Main Street was flooded with guests,
many running up the stairs to the Disneyland Railroad Station to
be the first ones aboard to circle the park. Many ran into my office,
thinking it was some kind of an exhibit, and I would say, "This is
the Guest Relations office, may I help you?" Some said, "Oh, we
thought there would be a show in here."

I had nothing on my schedule this day, so I left my office and
roamed the park to see people's reaction. One of the first negative
complaints I heard was, "Where are the water fountains?" I started
to think back to when I was filing those blueprints and recalled
seeing water fountains in the plans. Then I remembered the
plumbers' strike that limited the number that could be installed by
Opening Day. I heard some guest grumbling, "They did this on
purpose so we would have to buy soft drinks." This was, however,
simply not true. Walt would never have done something like that.

I bumped into Dad in Frontierland and he said, "You won't
believe what happened. At the snack shop at the end of New
Orleans Street, the plumbers mistakenly hooked up the outside
water sprinklers to the inside orange juice machine, and for a brief
period of time, the lawn was being watered with orange juice and
the customers were handed a tall glass of ice water!"

Other malfunctions happened at some of the other Lands, but
overall things performed as expected. One exception was complaints
about there being no benches for the park guests to sit and rest.
Many guests were sitting on the lawn areas around the Hub. I was
so accustomed to seeing the park with only a few people around

THE PARK'S lack of benches resulted in guests crashing wherever they could find some shade.

that it was exciting to see it filling that day with so many guests, mainly adults. The new park was something akin to a new car: it takes a little time to get the bugs out, and I knew that soon Walt would remedy all of the problems.

Fantasyland was a whirl with kids riding on the carousel and too much "whirl" on the Teacups, which caused some guests to lose their breakfast. Lines for guests grew long waiting to take the dark rides: Snow White, Peter Pan, and Mr. Toad's Wild Ride.

In Adventureland is where I heard the most praise. Some guests took the Jungle Boat ride three or four times. Many snapped countless pictures; others hung out at the Bazaar. On this first day, I thought Adventureland among all the Lands was the most beautiful and the most complete in its final touches.

Main Street was really looking and sounding like the Main Street of a real 1900s small town, with the ringing of the Penny Arcade, the "clop, clop" of the horses pulling the streetcars and the surreys, and the blowing of the Disneyland Railroad's train whistle as it left

JUNGLE CRUISE had the longest lines in the park.

the station. Dee Fisher, besides managing the Wurlitzer Music Company exhibit, was also a fine keyboardist and would play songs of that era on one of the shop's large organs. Bank of America was doing business, and Trinidad, in his whites, was keeping the streets clean of horse residue. I checked into my office, and Barbara said the nuns were arriving tomorrow at 10:00 A.M.

I had lunch at the Red Wagon Inn, after which I caught the show at the Golden Horseshoe. I was anxious to become familiar with it so I could best inform my future VIP's of what they would experience. It was shaping up quite well and running a lot smoother than before. In particular, Judy Marsh as Slue Foot Sue dazzled me. She was quite a sight to see. The band consisted of three musicians. Mel Patterson was the drummer, Shorty Sherock was the trumpet player, and Charles Lavere, a great piano player, rounded out the trio. I especially noticed Mel. He was sharp looking as well as a great drummer. He not only had to keep good time, but also had to use other instruments, such as a penny whistle, cowbell, and other sound effects to coincide with the performers' action. Overall, with Don Novis' singing, Wally Boag's comedy, and the four can can dancers, it was a great show.

I walked down Main Street, stopped at the outdoor flower shop next to the Carnation Ice Cream Parlor, and chatted with my sister, Bobbie. She loved working with the flowers and still does to this day. I proceeded on to the Maxwell House, to grab a cup of coffee and visit with Dad.

For the park's first week, I did not have much on my schedule, but tours were starting to be booked. Since I had no hosts under me at that time, I was to conduct all of the tours myself.

The first public tour I can recall occurred the second morning: a group of 60 nuns that arrived in a dozen limousines. This caused quite a bit of confusion at the Main Gate because they pulled in en masse instead of going to the reserved parking spaces. I quickly discovered that large groups were particularly challenging, trying to maneuver them through the crowds and explain the features of the park so they could hear me. At that time, we did not have the use of bullhorns. Fortunately, I succeeded in giving them a great time and Walt subsequently received a glowing thank you note.

The next few days were rather slow in the tour department, until an old high school friend was hired as Special Events Coordinator under Tommy Walker. Tommy was the head of Customer Relations and Special Events. My old friend's name was Bob Jani. When we met, we both said, "What a small world!" Bob was brilliant and created many events in the park, including the opening ceremonies of Tom Sawyer's Island, the Main Street Electrical Parade, and the Christmas Parade. He was truly the brains of the Special Events Department. It was Bob's idea to invite church choirs from all over the state to perform at the first Christmas celebration at the Christmas Bowl, the final resting place of the Main Street gazebo. I gave Bob his inauguration to the park, and he was overwhelmed yet anxious to get started on his many plans for upcoming events in the park.

On occasion, a tour on my schedule would bypass me due to

Pepsi-Cola Pepsi-Cola Presents

THE ORIGINAL & ONLY

GOLDEN HORSESHOE

TROUPE of ARTISTES

FEATURING

MR. DONALD NOVIS
The Silver Toned Tenor

MR. WALLY BOAG
"The Traveling Salesman" & Versatile Comedian

MISS JUDY MARSH

AS

Slue Foot Sue, Sweetheart of The Frontier

AND

THE GOLDEN HORSESHOE GIRLS

SHIRLEY TOWERS   GLENDA GUILFOYLE

GLORIA WATSON   SUSAN REED

AN EFFICIENT ORCHESTRA
Under The Capable Direction

OF

Dances & Terpsichore   **PROF. LaVERE**   Original Songs
Miss Theresa Allen   Mr. Tom Adair &
                                                      Mr. Charles LaVere

PROGRAMME

PART the FIRST

OVERTURE.................PROF. LaVERE & FULL ORCH.

OPENING —*"Hello Everybody"* ENTIRE & COMPLETE CAST

PART the SECOND

SONG —*"Bill Bailey"*........................JUDY MARSH

IRISH DITTY—*"Dear Old Donegal"*⎫
REFRAIN —*"Leprechaun Lullaby"* ⎬........DONALD NOVIS

BALLAD —*"Beautiful Dreamer"* DONALD NOVIS & CHORUS

COMICAL SONG —*"What Have We Here?"*....WALLY BOAG

LYRICAL LAMENT—*"Riverboat Blues"*⎫
SONG —*"A Lady Has To Mind Her* ⎬......JUDY MARSH
            P's And Q's"⎭

GRAND FINALE

SONGS —*"Pecos Bill"*
    & *"Offenbach's Can-Can"*..........ENTIRE COMPANY

Costumes by RENIÉ

MY FIRST souvenir program of the original Golden Horseshoe Revue.

some mistake in communication between Disneyland and the Studio. Such was the case with my first celebrity tour: Paul Whiteman, the "King of Jazz" of the 1920s and 1930s. When I realized that he had entered the park some twenty minutes earlier, I calculated that his group would have made it into the park about as far as the Hub area. Fortunately, that's exactly where he was. Being a jazz piano player as well as true jazz buff, I was looking forward to meeting him. So I had seen his picture many times and recognized him at once. I introduced myself and said I was sorry I had missed him at the front gate and offered my services. He said they would be OK on their own. I then mentioned my love of jazz and how I had enjoyed his earlier recordings, especially the ones with Bix Beiderbecke. Bix was the first white musician that the black musicians, who created jazz music at the turn of the 20th century, looked up to, including the great Louis Armstrong. When I mentioned Bix, a big smile came over Whiteman's face, and that opened up about twenty minutes of dialogue, since Bix was one of his very favorite members of the band. I did not want to waste his time, so I thanked him and said if he needed any help with his visit to contact me at the Police Station. He got a laugh at the name of my office.

Whenever a lull occurred between tours, I found myself getting into the habit of catching the next show at the Horseshoe. I would usually stand at the end of the bar near the stage, as I enjoyed not only hearing the music but got a kick watching the musicians perform, and, of course, watching Judy Marsh. I was really attracted to her, as was just about every executive in the park. She had that special personality that drew you to her.

I was starting to receive more calls from Walt's office regarding tours with some of the boss's special friends from his childhood. One of Walt's requests was to take them to the Golden Horseshoe. He enjoyed the show as well and would catch it whenever he could. It was standard procedure with these special guests, VIP's, celebrities and movie stars, to reserve box seats at either side of the stage. With the first group of Walt's friends, it was the first time I had seen the

CLOCK OF THE WORLD welcomed visitors to Tomorrowland.

show at such close proximity. Judy was even more beautiful at this distance, and knowing there were special people in the box, she would come very close and give a little bow during her routine.

Toward the end of the summer, the studio informed me of an important guest who would be arriving the next day. That guest was the great David O. Selznick, producer of *Gone with the Wind*. He was with his son. They were to have first class treatment, and I was to stay with them throughout the entire day. I met them the next morning and David was interested in everything from the very beginning of the tour. He was very impressed by the detailed architecture of Main Street along with the horse-drawn trolley and the surreys. He said it reminded him of his young days in New York. At the end of Main Street, looking towards the Hub, he found it a most interesting concept for an amusement park. We continued on

IN TOMORROWLAND, I gave movie producer David O. Selznick a tour of the Monsanto Hall of Chemistry.

to Tomorrowland until we reached the 360-degree Circarama screen show of a ride through Los Angeles. He was very impressed with this attraction.

As we gazed at the castle in Fantasyland, he said it was a most beautiful piece of work and very much defined the image of Walt. He liked the carnival atmosphere of Fantasyland. We proceeded on to Frontierland and he commented on the authentic appearance of

THOUGH SHORT-LIVED, horse-drawn surreys were a primary mode of transportation down Main Street during the park's first year.

the entrance. We took a ride on the Mark Twain, which he enjoyed, and was impressed with the detail of the riverboat. We stopped at the Golden Horseshoe. The studio said he did not want to take in the show as it would take up too much time, but I took him inside for a few minutes just to give him a peek at the show in progress. When we left, he said, "Maybe we should have taken the time, it looked like a great show." I assured him that it as. We proceeded down the wooden walkway and stopped at the Pendleton Woolen Mills shop, and was Bill Carpenter glad we did. As David liked what he saw, he purchased about $400.00 worth of merchandise. Occasionally his son would mention, "Jennifer would like this," or "Jennifer would love this." This reference was to the great star Jennifer Jones, who was David's wife. As our tour wound down, I asked if he would take a moment to meet Dad at the Maxwell House. He graciously agreed and they had a brief but enjoyable visit. I never realized what a giant he was in the motion picture industry until years later when I was in the industry myself. I actually worked in his Culver City studio office when I was hired on the Blake Edward's movie *Sunset*.

During this time, I was working six days a week, but still managed to get to Hermosa Beach one night a week to visit my old second home, the Lighthouse Cafe, one of the most popular jazz clubs in California. Before I was drafted into the Army, I practically lived at the club. I got to know Howard Rumsey, the leader of the band, known as the Lighthouse All Stars. Howard introduced me to the rest of the band—"Shorty" Rogers, trumpet; Jimmy Giuffre, tenor sax; Milt Bernhart, trombone; Shelly Manne, drums; and Frank Patchen, piano. Howard played the bass. I mention this part of my life because if it had not been for Shorty giving me a crash course on the trumpet six months before I was drafted, I would have never become a member of the 43rd Army band in Alaska. He literally saved me from combat in the Korean War, as I was in excellent physical shape and would have been stuck in the infantry. During those early times, I met my mentor on the piano, a natural self-taught genius, Hampton Hawes. He gave me a few lessons and we became close friends until his unfortunate early death at age 48 in 1977. (His lovely widow, Jacque Hawes, I continued to call my sister; we would get together and go out on the town to hear great jazz until her more recent passing.) All my friends in the band were proud of my position at Disneyland and I had them all out to the park as my guests.

The summer was just ending when I received a call from Dolores Voght, Walt's private secretary. A very special friend of Walt's would be arriving soon and I was to make sure to set aside two days of my schedule to devote to him. I was excited when she told me the friend was the maestro Leopold Stokowski, the great conductor of the score to *Fantasia*, Walt's animated movie tribute to classical music. Mr. Stokowski would be bringing his two small children from his

PRE-DISNEY, in my Army band uniform, a gig I owe to trumpeter Shorty Rogers.

marriage to Gloria Vanderbilt. The day arrived and I met them at the front gate. He was very tall and aged, 73 at the time. The children were about nine and ten years old. He asked if I would mind watching over the children for him. As they appeared to be well behaved children, I agreed and did not ask any questions. At the beginning of his visit, I could tell by the look on his face that he was in awe of what he was seeing. As we walked down Main Street at a slow pace with me holding a hand of each child and the statuesque elderly man following behind, many guests were attracted to him, apparently sensing he was someone famous, but not quite sure who he was. As we entered Adventureland, Mr. Stokowski said he would sit on a bench while I took the children on the Jungle Cruise, which they thoroughly enjoyed. We moved on to Frontierland, where we all boarded the Mark Twain, on which

ADVENTURELAND ENTRANCE beckoned explorers young and old.

Maestro could sit and enjoy the ride. I became aware why two days were scheduled for his visit as he tired easily and needed to rest often. As we left the Mark Twain, a mock gun fight broke out with Sheriff Lucky in hot pursuit of Black Bart. These gunbattles usually lasted about ten minutes and as the kids watched the action, they were mesmerized.

Barbara had made reservations for lunch in Walt's private dining room at the Red Wagon Inn. Mr. Stokowski really liked the atmosphere of the room. We placed our orders. I always selected their famous Shrimp Louie, and the staff always prepared a giant one for me. During lunch, we discussed the park, and Mr. Stokowski asked me about my interests in life. Of course, I said music. "What about music?" he inquired. "Tell me." When I told him of my love of jazz and classical music, and that I played and was studying the

JUNGLE CRUISE opened with seven boats, but quickly needed more to meet guest demand for the popular attraction.

piano, he wanted to know where I was studying. I replied that I was studying from private teachers. However, when I told him about my plans to study at the University of Mexico City, his face lit up. He said, "Bob, when you get ready to go there, let me know. I know a number of musicians and conductors of the symphony orchestra at the University of Mexico and I will tell them to take good care of you." I was touched at what he had just said, and I told him I was very grateful for him to feel that way about me. He had a twinkle in his eyes and said, "I love to help young musicians."

After lunch, I could see he was looking a little tired, but his lovely children were full of energy and asked Papa if they could ride in the jungle again. He said yes, if I would take them. I found him a bench

CAMERAS ARE being put into place for filming of and aboard the new Chicken of the Sea Pirate Ship.

where he could relax, and told him I would take the kids back to the jungle. After Adventureland, the Maestro called it a day, and we made plans to meet again the following morning.

The next day, we took the streetcar to the Hub, and it was definitely Fantasyland time for the kids. We walked around the plaza and entered through the castle. Before going in, we stopped and marveled at the sight of Sleeping Beauty Castle. Everyone I took through the castle entrance thought it was beautiful and was typically stunned at his or her first look, especially at night. Luckily, there was a bench near Merlin's Magic Shop. Mr. Stokowski said, "Take the kids on the rides, Bob. I'll sit here and watch as I am enjoying all of this." The kids and I went all through Fantasyland, including Casey Jr., all the dark rides, the Teacups, and finally King Arthur's Carrousel. While the kids were riding on the carousel, I checked on the Maestro. He was doing fine, enjoying watching his children having a great time. I sat next to him and asked him about conducting an orchestra. I said, "Maestro, how can you read a score as you conduct and how do you solve problems on a new composition?" (A score is the music written on large pages, that has every instrument and percussion sound, and you must be able to read at sight and hear everything instantly.) He said, "You learn by studying every instrument, then you take a score and read it over and over until you are familiar with every part of every instrument, as well as the whole percussion section. It takes many years to accomplish this. When I rehearse a new composition, and there is a problem spot that I cannot solve during rehearsal, often I will go to sleep with that problem on my mind and I will awaken during my sleep, and the solution comes to me. I will get up and make the correction on the score."

We left Fantasyland and walked to Tomorrowland. After a short time, Mr. Stokowski said it was time to leave, since he had to catch a flight to New York early that evening. We took the trolley down Main Street and disembarked right near my office. I had just received the first souvenir guide book of the park, and I asked if he would sign my copy. He was happy to comply with my request. Leopold Stokowski was not only one of the most interesting guests I had the privilege to accompany around the park, but was also the only one I ever asked for an autograph.

During the next couple of weeks, my tours consisted mainly of VIP's from various corporations, except for a Mr. Aden Smith, park superintendent for the state of Florida. He had spent time with Walt at the Studio, and my instructions were to make sure he and his entourage received the "red carpet treatment." The Golden Horseshoe Revue was a must-see for this group. I had Barbara make a reservation at the Red Wagon for lunch, and the Horseshoe later in the afternoon. When I had larger groups such as this one, they filled the box seats on stage left, so I would always take my spot at the end of the bar. It was from that location I could see the show and was closer to the band. By now, Mel Patterson, the drummer, would acknowledge me with a silent "hi" or a nod. I was becoming a familiar face there. We covered the rest of Frontierland and I felt that the party might want to finish the rest of the day on their own. They agreed with my suggestion, so I left them and went over to the Pavilion to see my friend Larry Alves, the assistant manager. Larry was an old friend from my senior class at Emeryville High School. He had come down to live in Southern California and Dad had secured him his job at the Pavilion. Larry plays a great tenor sax and we will get together to this day and play music.

I was not aware that Mel, from the Golden Horseshoe Revue, was a regular visitor to the Maxwell House and had become friends with Dad over many cups of coffee. Dad had told him of my love of jazz and of all the great musicians whom I not only studied with, but had become friends with, as well. Before Disneyland, Mel was a respected jazz drummer in the Orange County area. But since I was new to the area, I had never heard of Mel in Southern California's jazz circles. Although I had never spoken to Mel or even met him, he somehow had derived an insightful conclusion about me. One day, as I was standing on Main Street watching the guests pass by, Mel sidled up to me and said, "Have you turned on yet?" I said, "No, I haven't," and he said, "Are you ready to?" I said, "Sure," and I followed him out to the parking lot and got into his new Jaguar sports car. He passed me his pipe and said, "Have a poke." Needless to say, with all we had in common, we bonded and became lifelong friends.

Walt's office called and said Walt was coming out for the weekend, so I was to check his apartment and make sure everything was in order. I got the key from Kaye in City Hall and went through the back door in my office, took a right turn, and walked up to the apartment over the Fire Station. This was my first of many visits to Walt's private domain. As you entered the apartment, on the right was a huge liquor cabinet, which had its own key. The liquor cabinet

AUTOPIA miniature car ride was popular with the younger set.

formed a small hallway, which opened into a large living room extending to the right, and halfway down, on the right, was a wall extending to the end of the room with a door in the middle. That door led to the bathroom and a modern steam bath and shower. The furnishings were of priceless antiques and artwork hung on the flocked wallpapered walls. There was a large standing "disc music box" and a gold wire bird cage hanging near the window, with a little feathered bird on a swing. When wound it up, it would sing. The interior of the apartment reflected the turn of the century, just like the rest of Main Street. Authenticity carried even into Walt's apartment.

6

Hi Yo Silver! The Lone Ranger rides again—only this time it was to Disneyland! However, he was detained at the Main Gate until I arrived and accompanied him up Main Street. Clayton Moore, who played the masked lawman on TV, arrived in costume with his assistant (or it might have been his manager). There was a clause in Moore's contract stating that no matter where he appeared, he always had to wear the black mask. He was a nice man and stayed in character throughout the tour.

He walked through the park in a cautious manner, almost as if he was entering a hostile old town in an episode from his weekly TV program. We would stop occasionally and he would sign an autograph for a fan. It was one of the shortest tours I conducted, because he only wanted to see the park without riding any of the attractions. I think we did his visit in about 90 minutes, but during that time, he certainly did attract a lot of attention. He thanked me for my expertise in guiding him through another adventure and soon he was off into the sunset.

It was the beginning of November that I had my first "host" assigned to my office. His name was John Miller and he was the younger brother of Ron Miller, the great football star from the University of Southern California and later a star with the Los Angeles Rams. Ron was Walt's son-in-law, married to Diane Disney. John was the "black sheep" of the Miller family, very different from Ron and his father, John Sr., who managed the huge warehouse in the park off the service road. John was somewhat wild and had various jobs in the park working on the different rides in all the Lands. He was also known for his many escapades. One in particular occurred one night, as the park was closing. He told the ride operators in Fantasyland that Walt said it was OK for them to keep the rides operating after closing as he had some friends coming by who were still in a party mood. There were about six or seven in the party, mostly girls. Well, the operators took his word for it, and continued running the rides. When the park was empty, they all stripped down to nothing and partied for about an hour before calling it a night. The word around the park was that the party had gotten pretty wild.

John was younger than I was and we got along quite well. He seemed to have respect for me, and I think he realized that his new position in the park had some importance, as I told him this was serious work, since we were representing Walt to the special guests as well as the general public.

I gave him a little training, and he adapted to his new job well, because he was already familiar with the park. All I had to do was refine him a bit, and help him with his attire. It was a big help to have John as an assistant, because he did well in handling the tours I assigned to him and it gave me more time to spend with the more important tour groups.

My life was becoming quite busy. In addition to working six days a week, I met a nice woman who worked in the accounting office. Her name was Audrey Blasdel, and she was a fun lady. We had some great times together but she lived in Long Beach, about a 45-minute drive from the park. I was still living with my family in a lovely new home ten minutes from the park, so our getting together in the evening took up a lot of time. We were together for a couple of months, but my music studies and playing some gigs at the Banker's Club in San Bernardino at night, took up most of my time so we had a parting of the ways and ended our relationship. Fortunately, it was a friendly separation and we remained friends.

The 90-minute drive to San Bernardino was actually quite enjoyable for me, as, through my association with Audrey, I had become acquainted with her boss, Larry Tryon, who was the head of finance for the studio. Larry was a great person and drove a beautiful blue 1951 MG TD convertible sports car with a white top

DISNEYLAND DRIVER :

PLEASE LEAVE LINCOLN IN ADMINISTRATION

BUILDING PARKING AREA AND GIVE THE KEYS

TO RECEPTIONIST IN THAT BUILDING FOR

BOB D'ARCY.

Marian Clement
Walt's office

OCCASIONALLY part of my job included picking up VIP's in the company car.

and a rear tire cover. The car was the rage amongst the younger generation and Larry's was up for sale. I asked him the selling price and he quoted me $1,000.00, which, at that time, was a lot of money to me. I told him I only had about $400.00 saved and he said I could have the car using my $400.00 as a down payment and I could pay the balance off at $75.00 a month. I was happy, as I loved the car. The drive to the Banker's Club took me through a number of small canyons, which sports cars were built for, as much of the terrain of Europe is similar.

Disneyland's first Christmas was about six weeks away and Bob Jani stopped by with his plans for the Christmas Bowl. He was in the process of contacting about 300 church choirs that would be singing throughout the season. Bob thought "large scale" in most of his events. My part in the project was to help meet the choir groups at the main gate, escort them to the bowl, and position them off stage until it was their turn to perform. I was also to take turns with Bob and Cap Blackburn in announcing them over the microphone, which could be heard throughout the park. Bob would

DISNEYLAND BAND leader Vesey Walker (far right) was the father of my direct superior, Tommy Walker.

announce for one hour, and then I would do the same for the next hour, then Cap, which gave us each a two-hour break.

Walt told Tommy Walker that he was looking for something spectacular for the first Christmas celebration. Tommy asked Bob if he had any ideas on this. Bob had just started on the church choir event when he was called out of town. On the return flight, he did a rough sketch of ideas, one of which he titled "Disneyland's Christmas Parade." I did not know Bob had done this. Tommy had taken Bob's notes, copied them verbatim, and submitted "his" idea to Walt. It was a huge success and Tommy took all the credit, never even thanking Bob, and Walt thought it was all Tommy's idea. Bob, being such a nice, quiet man, told me about this and never got angry or upset. He just smiled and said, "Oh, well, I guess he just needed my help."

Tommy Walker was part of the University of Southern California group that had been recruited by Ron Miller. Tommy brought in his father, Vesey Walker, as the first leader of the Disneyland marching band. I became acquainted with some of the band members, and they loved their job, as good steady work was uncommon for a musician. However, they were not happy with Vesey. He was dull, strictly business, and no fun or humor was allowed. I do not say that they all felt that way, but from the members I met, it seemed to be the feeling of most of the band. I met Vesey only once, but I felt the same way. Tommy's behavior was similar to his father's, just not quite as intense. I sensed unfriendly vibes from him, but since I was working under his supervision (Guest Relations was a small part of Customer Relations), I shrugged them off and went on with my work.

Teresa Wright, a great actress of the Forties and Fifties, was another lovely woman whom I had the pleasure of escorting around the park. Teresa was brilliant in a classic suspense movie of the 1940s called *Shadow of a Doubt* with Joseph Cotten. She also starred in one of my very favorite movies when I was a young lad, called *Pride of the Yankees*. It was the story of Lou Gehrig, the great New York Yankees first baseman, starring Gary Cooper, with Teresa Wright playing his wife. As a kid, Lou Gehrig was my idol and I wanted to become a baseball player when I grew up. My Dad's second cousin was Joe McCarthy, one of the Yankees' greatest managers.

Teresa had four of her woman friends with her, and we all bonded right from the start.

Teresa and her friends were very upbeat and we had many laughs. Of course, I had Barbara book us for the afternoon show at the Golden Horseshoe. We sat in the box, stage left. During Judy's routine, she came over to us and made her customary bow and, in a low voice, said, "*Hello* there" to me. I got a warm feeling from this unexpected encounter, and Teresa said, "I think she likes you, Bob."

SINGER JUDY MARSH as Slue Foot Sue in the Golden Horseshoe Revue stole the show–and my heart.

I do not recall my reply, but I do know that I wanted to meet Judy personally. We continued hitting the highlights of the park, and we became more familiar with one another. Her friends were Mary, Terry, Stacey and Betty. What a great group of gals; they made it one of the most enjoyable tours I had experienced in my tenure at Disneyland. About a week later, they sent me a lovely card in a package with two fine classical recordings on the Angel Label, one of the most expensive LP's at that time.

Mel and I were getting together more frequently. We would meet at the Carnation Ice Cream Parlor for lunch or the Maxwell House for coffee and visit with Dad. He would stop by my office and when Barbara was on a break, we would go out the back door, down the service road, visit Blinky, and have a "poke."

Another tour that got away—and one that I had really been looking forward to—was Frank Sinatra. I had first heard him sing in 1941 on the radio show *Your Hit Parade*. I followed his career throughout the years, purchasing his albums. Frank was not only a wonderful singer with his rich tone, but he also loved jazz. On all of his recordings, he utilized all the best jazz and studio musicians. I think if he had brought his children with him, we would have connected. Why he did not bring his children, I will never know. The front gate was to notify me when he arrived. When the scheduled time came, I waited about ten minutes, then called the gate. They said, "Bob, he arrived and didn't wait; he went right on through and headed towards Main Street." I dashed from my office and headed for the Hub and there he was, looking around at the entrances to the Lands. I was preparing to approach him but he spun around, headed back down Main Street, and left the park. I was disappointed as it would have been a treat to talk music and the big band days with him.

Thanksgiving was here, and that was a family "stay-at-home" day. I went home early and Mom had prepared a great dinner. We all gave thanks for a fabulous feast and thanks for being a part of Disneyland.

Bob Jani came by with the list of all the choirs that would be participating in the Christmas Bowl, along with the schedule. What a chore! Bob had it so organized that it was clear to me it would all run smoothly. The groups would begin arriving during the first part of December and would perform through New Year's.

Teresa Wright

We hope you'll enjoy these records half as much as we enjoyed our day at Disneyland.

With the warmest thanks and best wishes from, — Mary, Terry Stacy, Betty & Teresa

A TREASURED thank-you card from Teresa Wright and her entourage.

7

It was during the holidays that Mel invited me to his house for dinner. Mel's family was upper middle class. His father had the distributorship for Pepsi-Cola for all of Orange County. This was Mel's connection into the band at the Golden Horseshoe. His wife, Ann, a lovely woman, was always stylishly dressed. Their son, Michael, was about nine years old, well mannered, and very mature for his age. Their house was large and well maintained. Ann was a great cook, an immaculate housekeeper and, like Mel, was a lot of fun to be around, both of them having warm personalities. After dinner, we got to know one another a bit better and, of course, listened to jazz. Mel had a great collection of jazz LP's, some from my gang from the Lighthouse All Stars. Before Disneyland, Mel was a working musician and had a steady gig at one of the finest men's clothiers in Santa Ana, a city close to Anaheim. He was a very sharp dresser, and between Mel and Dad, I picked up my style of attire, as my job at the park required me to look well groomed at all times.

The decorations were now in place for Christmas, and a walk around the park was a remarkable sight as the twinkling lights turned the evening into a sparkling wonderland, and the spirited musical voices of the choirs added a festive touch to the celebration.

As the various choir groups arrived at the front gate, I ushered them to the Christmas Bowl, creating a mini parade. I enjoyed announcing each group before their performances and got a kick out of hearing my voice amplified throughout the park. Rotating every hour did not make it seem like a chore as we each had a two-hour break in between announcements. At one point, I met Mel leaving the Golden Horseshoe after a show, and he said, "Have you got some time to join me? I'm going over to the Disneyland Hotel."

As I had a couple of free hours, he said, "Great! An old bartender friend of mine just started working there. Have you ever had a margarita?" I had never sampled this particular cocktail and Mel assured me that I would enjoy it as his friend made the best ones around. A margarita at that time consisted of tequila and Cointreau triple sec served on the rocks in a glass with the rim dipped in lime and salt. The cocktail back then was called the "Mexican martini."

After three cocktails, I told Mel I needed to head back to the park as my turn at the mic was about to begin. I was feeling good, but not drunk by any means, and I strolled into the Bowl right on time to begin my introductions. Our written dialogue was, "Good evening, ladies and gentlemen and children. Welcome to the Christmas Bowl!" I would then announce the town and church that was being represented. The margaritas were kicking in by this time and I said, "Good evening, ladies and gentlemen and children. Welcome to the Hollywood Bowl—er, excuse me, the Christmas Bowl," and continued announcing the choir to perform. There was mild laughter at my goof. The Bowl was filled to capacity that evening and after my hour had ended, I noticed that Walt and his wife Lillian were seated in the very last bench. I froze, looked at Walt, and started to apologize. He stopped me and said, "Kid (he always called me Kid), I like the way you think big," and gave me a smile. I felt a great sense of relief as they all laughed.

In addition to Sheriff Lucky and Black Bart, there was another character in Frontierland who was popular with the guests. He was a tall, colorful Indian who roamed the Painted Desert and would stop at certain spots and strike a pose on top of his beautiful horse. His name was Eddie Little Sky. I became acquainted with Eddie, and we would share conversation over breakfast at Aunt Jemima's. One morning he related an incident he had earlier experienced: "I came to work early and was walking my horse. Before I started my performance, I noticed a man walking through an unauthorized area and I yelled for him to get out, that this was a restricted space. As I bumped into him, I apologized for being so gruff. He said, 'Oh, that's all right, you were just doing your job. I respect you for

GUEST BANDS frequently played in front of the Opera House on Main Street, with yours truly as the announcer.

that.' He then shook my hand and said, 'Nice to meet you. I'm Walt Disney.' As he walked away, I realized who I had just encountered... Walt Disney, a down to earth genius."

I remained quite busy with the choirs and tours with VIP's from our state government and more of Walt's personal friends. I was having lunch at Carnation when Mel joined me. During our conversation, he mentioned that he had come to know Judy pretty well and thought we would make a good match. When he suggested that I ask her out, I replied that I was surely at the very end of a long line of guys interested in her. He suggested that I give the idea

AMONG THE guest band leaders was the oldest brother of jazz great Dave Brubeck, Henry Brubeck, who is seen here shaking my hand.

some thought and added that she was only attracted to certain types of men. As I considered his suggestion, the thought of being with her excited me, and from what Mel had said, I thought I had a shot of getting a date with her.

The park was doing a brisk business, as were the shops and restaurants. The choirs added to the music agenda along with the Disneyland Band marching up and down Main Street playing carols, and the Christmas parade was a big hit as well. Disneyland's first Christmas was a big success, and I was getting some gigs playing special events at the Disneyland Hotel, which included a booking for a large party on New Year's Eve.

Once the holidays were over, the park settled down to a more relaxed pace. Walt had been involved in the development of Alpine Village in the Lake Tahoe area in preparation for the Winter Olympics. During the first week of the new year, Walt and most of the executives went up to Lake Tahoe to oversee the development of the project. The Sunday morning guest count was low and the park was moving in slow motion. If any problems should develop, security was to call my office and I would handle the situation. Barbara was off this day and John and I were sitting around with little to keep us occupied. During the late morning, in an attempt to beat the boredom, John suggested we visit Walt's apartment upstairs. John's next suggestion was that we should have a cocktail, yet neither one of us had a key to the liquor cabinet. So John pulled out his pocketknife and popped open the door. We could see there was a complete stock of liquor and I thought that maybe we were on the path to destruction. This was a clear case of "breaking and entering" into some very private property, but, for some reason, neither John nor I had any fear. We mixed ourselves a cocktail and then John suggested we invite some friends to join us. We got on the phone and called some friends, mostly women, from the various restaurants and a few ride operators he knew.

Everyone in the park wanted to see what Walt's apartment looked like so we partied and had a great time. We all agreed that we would never forget that party as we carried on until almost midnight. The girls cleaned up, John "re-secured" the liquor cabinet, we locked up the apartment, and went home.

The next morning, Monday, I arrived at the office a little late with a slight hangover. John had not arrived at work yet when Barbara advised me that Dolores, from Walt's office at the Studio, had called. All the executives were back at the park and word had spread about our party. Barbara gave me a look that indicated I was in big trouble. I started to clear out my desk, thinking a "pink slip" was next, when the phone rang. Barbara handed me the phone and indicated that it was Dolores. As I took the call, I told Dolores that

I was packing up my desk and would be leaving shortly. She replied that when she learned of the party, she notified Walt that John Miller and Bob D'Arcy had hosted quite a party in his apartment yesterday that lasted well into the night. In attendance were a number of the girls who worked in the park. Walt inquired about the condition of the apartment and whether any damage had occurred. Dolores replied that there was no evidence that a party had been held there. Walt replied, "Hat's off to them, they have a lot of guts, I like that." How could you not love Walt? What CEO today would be so understanding and actually be amused about two clowns in the lower echelon committing such a cardinal sin? I often wondered who snitched on us, but I did not ask Dolores. It must have been my friend Kaye in City Hall who gave us a clean bill of health on the pristine condition of the apartment. Whenever Walt came to the park, he had to pass by my office to get to his apartment. On those occasions, he would drop in and compliment me for doing a good job of escorting his friends or dignitaries through the park. He never mentioned the party. I was certain he would have pulled me aside and given me a few stern words. It was another side of Walt that gave me such tremendous respect for him.

Shortly after the infamous party, I received a memo stating that I had received a nice raise in salary. That morning I received a call from Fran, C.V. Wood's secretary. She said C.V. wanted to see me in his office right now, if I was not busy. I thought, "What did I do now?," since C.V. never called me to his office. Upon my arrival, Fran, a very pretty woman, had a smile on her face as she told me to go on into his office. C.V. said, "Bubba, sit down. I got word of your raise, and this calls for a drink." He went over to his bar, mixed us a scotch and soda, toasted me, and said, "Bob, you're doing a great job in your department. Many of my friends that you have escorted through the park have told me how much they enjoyed your company, and I have not had the time to thank you until now. Keep up the great image of Disneyland." I assured him that I felt so lucky to have the greatest job in the park. As we shook hands, he replied, "And you deserve it."

DISNEYLAND. INC.
EMPLOYEE STATUS CHANGE ADVICE

☒ RATE	
☐ CLASSIFICATION	
☐ TRANSFER	D'Arcy, Robert W.
☐ SHIFT	
☐ VACATION	532 Pine Way Anaheim
☐ LEAVE OF ABSENCE	
☐ OTHER	462-44-8479

DATE 1-12-56
EFF. DATE 1-16-56
PAYROLL STATUS
☒ HOURLY
☒ SALARIED

FACTORS	FROM	TO
CLASSIFICATION & CODE	Guest Relation Ass't. B	Same
DEPARTMENT NAME & NO.	Guest Relations #64	Same
SHIFT	(as scheduled)	Same
RATE	$1.70 p/h	$1.80
TRANSFER APPROVALS		
ADDITIONAL DATA		

26 Week Review

APPROVED:	APPROVED:	APPROVED:	PERSONNEL APPROVAL

DAYS AFTER park VP C.V. Wood granted me a raise, he found himself out of a job.

As I walked back to my office, I almost had to pinch myself. I had only been out of the Army for one year and all this had happened to me. Then, on January 19, 1956, Walt issued a formal memo to all department heads that C.V. had submitted his resignation as Vice President and General Manager of Disneyland to form his own company, Telesearch, Inc. His new company would be involved in research and marketing of television programs. I had a feeling of sadness at his departure for not only did he treat me with decency, but also he was very popular with all of the executives. At that time, Walt assumed C.V.'s duties and did not hire a new General Manager.

Despite the turmoil at the top, financial reports showed the park in good shape. Park management issued a statement, which revealed that 2,006,362 visitors had been to Disneyland in its first six months. The attendance figure was within three percent of the number estimated before the park opened the previous summer. Of this total, 35 percent (or 700,000) visitors had come from outside of the State of California, thus making Disneyland the largest single attraction in the West. Out-of-state visitors included people from all 48 states, U.S. territories, and 63 foreign countries. Most interestingly, adults outnumbered children by a ratio of four to one. Average per capita spending for all visitors was $2.29. This sum included everything except food.

The week ending January 1, 1956, was the second largest attendance week in the park's history, surpassed only by opening week. Attendance for the Christmas week was 151,425 visitors.

Disneyland management also noted that the past six months had been the largest tourist months in the history of Southern California, according to the All Year Club of Southern California. Research interviews with visitors conducted within the park on a regular basis, pointed out that Disneyland played a prominent part in influencing decisions by out-of-state visitors to visit Southern California and, thus, aided the Southland's entire tourist industry.

During Disneyland's constructions phase, Walter Knott, operator of Knott's Berry Farm, contacted Walt Disney. Knott's Berry Farm was a very small, but interesting, attraction with a one street western town and a great restaurant. It was famous for its fried chicken dinners, as well as its jams and jellies. Walter Knott was concerned that his attraction might suffer a great revenue loss because of the competition with Disneyland. Walt Disney, being a great visionary, predicted that Knott's Berry Farm would not only do more business, but would become a much larger enterprise. His predictions were accurate, as Knott's Berry Farm became a major Southern California tourist attraction.

8

I met a Mr. Larry Landsburg, Walt's producer in Mexico. Ed Ettinger's office set up his visit and asked me to spend about an hour briefly showing him the layout of the park, taking him to Tomorrowland to see the Circarama exhibit, and then letting him on his own. As I was returning to the Hub, I saw Mel coming out of Frontierland after the show. He said, "I was going to your office. Ann asked me to invite you over for dinner this Saturday night. If you can make it, she's cooking up something special." I told him I was free and would enjoy that very much.

I went over around 7:00 P.M., Ann answered the door, and I could smell the aroma of a prime rib being roasted. As I entered, I could not believe what I saw. There was Mel and Judy standing with smiles on their faces. Mel said, "Come on in' man, it's going to be a fun evening." Judy took my hand and said, "We finally get to meet after all this time." I responded, "I can't believe this is happening." We all laughed, Ann fixed me a drink, and we had a nice short visit before the delicious dinner.

After dinner, we adjourned to the living room. Mel put on some swinging music, and, after Michael went to bed, we all had a "poke" on Mel's pipe. A lot of dialogue followed, intermixed with sometimes uncontrollable laughter. It was just a great evening of getting to know each other, topped off with peach cobbler a la mode out of Ann's oven. What wonderful friends I had to do such a lovely thing for me. I will never forget that night. We said goodnight with a warm thank you from Judy and me. I walked Judy to her car, we hugged for what seemed like forever, and she gave me a short but warm kiss. She was so beautiful up close like this and I could barely get out the words: "When can we meet again?" She said, "I'm free

DISNEYLAND was among the publicity stops for Air Force Sgt. Richard H. Holden, an Alaskan Air Command jet aircraft technician, and his wife, Roberta, after he was named Airman of the Year in the first annual contest sponsored by Northrup.

every night after the last show." I asked, "Is tomorrow night too soon?" and she said, "I'll be waiting for you."

The next day, I had a group from Northrop Aircraft Corporation. This was a special tour, since they were honoring the Air Force's Airman of the Year, Sergeant Holden, and his wife, plus their photographer. We took our time visiting all the main attractions and, of course, the Golden Horseshoe, which now had a completely different meaning to me. Mel gave me a big smile and said, "Hi," and Judy gave her bow to us in the box and a very bright smile to me. We ended at Aunt Jemima's. The whole tour was captured on 16mm film as well as in many still shots. The film was shown to the Air Force brass in Washington, D.C.—another neat little promotion for Disneyland.

That night I met Judy and I felt so proud walking down Main Street. I even carried her make-up kit. We decided to have a drink at the Disneyland Hotel. We relaxed and talked about each other's favorite things in life, especially music. When we returned to her car, we made a date for the following day, as we were both off on Monday. I said, "Good night," and this time we shared a long warm kiss and she gave me directions to her rented house near the park.

I picked her up the next morning around 10:00 A.M. She really liked my MG and we took a long, pleasant ride through many orange and avocado groves. Orange County in those days was beautiful. The population was sparse; there were many big farms, with rows and rows of fruit trees and neat-looking homes tucked away in the rear. We arrived in Newport Beach, headed south to Laguna Beach, and had a long leisurely lunch. The town of Laguna Beach was a clean, interesting village atmosphere with a lot of shops and art galleries. We had fun strolling about. Around late afternoon, we drove home. The ride was so much fun in the MG and we had many laughs. When we arrived at her house, she said, "I want you to come over this Sunday after work and I'll cook a nice dinner for us, and we'll have a fun, relaxed evening." That was something I looked forward to throughout the next week.

President Sukarno of Indonesia was my first tour of the week, along with his entourage. It was a large group that attracted attention because they were in uniform—khaki with black and red accents. The President especially liked Adventureland; his interpreter said it reminded him of home. They were a happy lot.

Dolores called and told me to be ready the next day to receive a

DISNEYLAND, INC.

INTER-OFFICE COMMUNICATION

Date __March 20, 1956__

To___Ronnie Scheuller___ From___Bev Palombo___

Subject___

Dolores, Walt's secretary, called and gave us the following information:

Marks Leva, his wife and two children, will arrive at 11:00 A.M. Sunday, March 25th. Could Bob d'Arcy meet them at the main gate with the enclosed passes. Dollores suggested that Bob take them to lunch (we are to pay) and then start them off on a tour, giving them suggestions as to what they might want to do and see. They will probably want to be on their own once he starts them off.

Mr. Leva is the former Ass't. Secretary of Defense under Forrestal.

Bev

Encl. (4)

MEMO ALERTED us of a special tour for Marx Leva (erroneously referred to as "Marks," who was Assistant Secretary of Defense had framed much of the legislation that unified the United States' armed services after World War II.

special party arriving about 11:00 A.M., a Mr. Marx Leva, his wife, and two children. Mr. Leva was the former assistant to the first U.S. Secretary of Defense, James Forrestal. We spent a lot of time with his kids in Fantasyland and Frontierland and I took them on the Mark Twain. As usual with dignitaries, I led them up to the pilot's cabin. This particular day, my brother Ron was the acting skipper. He was a real character, kind of on the wild and crazy side, who liked to clown around with the guests, especially when he piloted the Mark Twain. I introduced my guests to him, not revealing that he was my brother. Ron said, "Nice to meet you," then with a puzzled look on his face, added, "How did you get stuck with this host? Usually with special guests like you, the head of Guest Relations takes them on their tour." He then broke into a big laugh and said, "You really got stuck with a clown. He's my brother." As

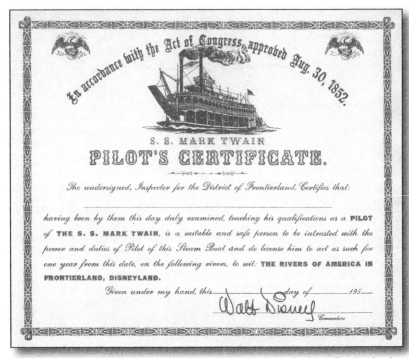

KIDS AND special guests lucky enough to be invited to tour the Mark Twain wheelhouse received a Pilot's Certificate as a memento.

we rounded the first right turn, my guests commented on Walt's great imagination, at which time Ron agreed, "He has a very wonderful imagination. Look at those ducks out there, they look so real." Mr. Leva asked, "Are they animated?" "Oh, yeah," Ron replied. Just then the ducks flew away. We all laughed, and I said, "Meet Ron, the real clown of the family!"

Ron's job was unique as he was one of the only employees who worked all the rides. Mosts of the other ride operators were assigned to work one ride only. When Ron came to work, he never knew where he would be until he checked his timecard and went to wardrobe to suit up for whatever Land he would be working in. Sometimes he worked two or three different rides in one day and would have to make the appropriate changes. One particular day in Fantasyland, he was helping a young woman get on a horse on the carousel when her pants split. Being Mr. Suave, Ron took his coat off, covered her damaged area, and escorted her to wardrobe, where they stitched up her pants.

Ron's favorite assignment was Frontierland and he became good friends with Sheriff Lucky. When Ron's shift was over, he would assist Lucky on his security duties after the park closed. They would make the rounds of all the shops to make sure they were locked up, kind of like Festus on the television show *Gunsmoke*. Ron said he really felt like he was living the "Old West Days."

Ron also spent time with Wally Boag, listening to his stories of the old times in show business. Before he worked for Disneyland attractions, he worked with Dad, helping service the concessions Dad oversaw, which included serving Donald Duck orange juice and Welch's grape juice throughout the park.

My youngest brother, Jim, was one of Disneyland's first newspaper boys, selling the *Disneyland News* on Main Street during his summer vacation. With my sister, Bobbie, selling flowers at the Flower Market next to Carnation on Main Street, the D'Arcys were all over Disneyland. The only one missing was my dear older brother, Dave, who long ago had moved to Ephrata, Washington.

One of the great challenges about my job was the variety of guests I had to deal with. Besides movie stars, dignitaries, foreign heads of state and U.S. government officials, there were just down-to-earth people who, through whatever channels, received special tours of the park.

Dorothy Manes put one such tour together. Dorothy was the first lady executive of Disneyland, in charge of group sales. She came to Disneyland from Oakland, California, where she was the Director of Children's Fairyland, on the city's famous Lake Merritt, which lies in the center of the city. Since Oakland was the city where I was born and where Dad had been a city council member, I suspect Dad had something to do with Dorothy being hired, but I could be wrong. Anyways, Dorothy and I became great friends, and she had a great respect for Dad. This tour was special as it was for a little boy named Paul, who had been diagnosed as suffering from a rare blood disease. Paul was seven years old and his little sister, Betsy

Lou, was five. The children's father had contacted someone at the Studio, they turned the inquiry over to Dorothy and me, and Dorothy prearranged everything in the different Lands. There was a clown waiting for them on the Mark Twain. Jimmy Clark, who played the piano in the Golden Horseshoe before the main show to warm up the guests, brought the kids up to the piano and sang to them. The kids called me "Uncle Bob" and Dorothy became "Aunt Dotty." Betsy fell in love with Jimmy Clark and Paul fell in love with my Judy as Slue Foot Sue. The kids took such a liking to Dorothy and me that they held our hands everywhere we went. Paul got to lead the Disneyland marching band, they took all the rides, and got pilot's licenses on the Mark Twain. All in all, it was very touching the way they called Dorothy and me by our new names and gave us many hugs throughout the tour. They talked to us as if we were their real aunt and uncle.

They did not want to leave, but, after one last big hug, they were gone. The father wrote Walt a very long thank you letter and his secretary, Dolores, said Walt was proud of us.

9

Sunday finally arrived. After work, I headed home, showered, put on fresh clothes, got in the MG, and departed for Judy's. I was greeted with a warm embrace and a familiar kiss. She mixed us a cocktail, we touched glasses, and she continued to prepare our dinner. Besides all of her lovely charms, Judy was a gourmet chef. She had done some of the preparations the previous night, so all she had to do now was tend to the roast beef and make a fresh salad. The table was set with two pink candles glowing in the dimly lit dining room. The living room was off to the side, keeping with the amiable atmosphere. The music was from one of my favorite albums—one side was West Coast jazz, and the other side was East Coast jazz. We were listening to "Autumn Leaves" from the East, a long, beautifully arranged ballad that was very romantic. Dinner was not quite ready so we went to the living room, sat on the couch, enjoyed the music, and finished our cocktails. As we held hands, I had a most comfortable feeling of being "at home." I would learn later that Judy was a true homebody.

The meal was superb. She really knew her way with food; everything was prepared just right. I helped her clear the table and she said the dishes could wait. As we returned to the living room, she put on another album of soft ballads. Soon we were in each other's arms for a long time for short kisses, long kisses, and Eskimo kisses. Laughing in between, I would mention something that would amuse us both. One of the many experiences we had in common was a great sense of humor. She had the most infectious laugh that tended to put me in a great mood. We took a break from our passion and she served pistachio ice cream, which became our favorite, but only the Green Lantern brand would do. After another short kiss, she indicated that after she changed her attire that she would like to dance for me. I was on an emotional high, as I had never had this experience before. When she emerged from her bedroom, to say she appeared beautiful would be an understatement; a more appropriate description would be "exotic." She was attired in a very sheer light pink gown with a paler pink bra and panties underneath. After a most sensual performance, the music ended and as she glided onto my lap she softly asked, "How did you like that?" As I replied how much I had enjoyed her performance and indicated how very beautiful she was, she said, "You know, babe, you don't have to go home tonight." I didn't.

I love the smell of fresh coffee brewing in the morning. Not only was the aroma of coffee in the air, so were the tempting smells of bacon, eggs and toast. As Judy greeted me with "Good morning, sleepyhead," she gave me a kiss and a steaming cup of hot coffee. We shared the tasty breakfast, which was topped off by fresh cantaloupe. I said I had better call Mom, because I had never missed a night at home before and I did not want her to be concerned. Judy said she would love to meet her. After chatting with Mom, I helped Judy with the dishes and we proceeded to my house.

As we visited over coffee, Judy and Mother bonded right away. Mother enjoyed Judy's relaxed personality and indicated that, after seeing her performance at the Golden Horseshoe, she appeared just as bright in person as she had on stage. After coffee, I showed Judy my bedroom. When I opened the door, she broke out in laughter. My bedroom was comprised of my bed and a six-foot-eight-inch Baldwin Parlor grand piano. She questioned how I had been able to get the piano into the bedroom. I explained that I had purchased my piano from a large company in Los Angeles and, upon delivery, they had removed the legs, turned the piano onto its side, rolled it in on a dolly, and then reassembled the legs once it was in my bedroom. Judy asked me to play a tune for her. I chose "All the Things You Are," the great Jerome Kern composition. After I had finished, she said, "I would like to sing it with you." So I gave her an "intro" and we made music together.

PUBLICITY PHOTO for Judy Marsh.

I was just beginning to study music seriously. I was not nearly as accomplished as Judy, but, fortunately, she sang all the songs in the keys in which they were written, which happened to be the keys I was familiar with. She liked the way I played and we spent much of the afternoon going through my repertoire. What fun we had! While we were enjoying our afternoon, Dad had returned home. After our music session, we returned to the dining room to find

THROUGH THE SPRING I welcomed dozens of guest bands to perform at the park.

Dad with a big smile on his face, remarking, "So, this is what Slue Foot Sue does on her day off." I introduced Judy to Dad, and she responded with a big hug. Dad was from New York and in his younger days was a professional singer with the then-famous Empire State Quartet. He said he was enjoying our music and asked when we were going to form our own group, at which Judy just laughed and replied, "We just did!" After a short visit with Mother and Dad, we excused ourselves to enjoy a drive to finish our wonderful afternoon. When I walked Judy to her front door, I thanked her for the most beautiful experience of my life. She replied, "The pleasure was all mine." Before we kissed goodbye, we just gazed into each

MORE YOUNG musicians at a festival of high school bands.

other's eyes. At this moment, I realized what love was all about—the way she could excite me, love me, make me laugh, and make me feel so comfortable. I had never known such a lovely soul before. We did not have to make a date after our goodnight kiss; she just said, "See you tomorrow at the park."

Disneyland's first Easter celebration was a week away. One of the highlights was an Easter egg hunt at the flagpole on Main Street for kids aged five and under. The child finding the "Golden Egg" would receive special prizes with the grand prize being able to spend the whole day with Walt Disney himself.

Dolores called me and said that Walt would like me to purchase

EVEN MORE BANDS.

a large Easter lily and a colorful Easter card and write a little message inside, which he would sign later, for Lillian. When Mrs. Disney arrived at the apartment for the weekend, the flowers and card would be waiting for her. I truly felt honored to have Walt ask me to perform a task of such a personal nature for him.

Walt had so many friends, and it seemed as though I escorted all of them through the park. They were always the nicest people and, knowing they were close friends of Walt made these tours even more

Bob D'Arcy

Mr. & Mrs. Prieto and their two daughters, Georgina and Esther - personal friends of Walt Disney. They are from Mexico City. He is a business man & attorney associated with Amaconda Wire & Cable which is a subsidiary of Amaconda Copper.

Give them the royal treatment. Stay with them as long as they are in the Park. Take them to lunch. Everything on the house.

Will be in between 11:00 and 12:00 noon.

OLYMPIC FENCER Eduardo Prieto and his family were close friends of Walt's and to be given "the royal treatment."

special for me. My biggest reward from these experiences came when Walt would drop by my office and tell me how happy he was that his friends had had such a great visit and that my work was appreciated. He told me that he had received many letters of thanks and my name would always be mentioned. He would say, "You're doing a great job, kid. Keep up the good work." Dad was so accurate in his assessment of Walt Disney—when you worked hard and enjoyed your job, he was your friend.

I had the privilege of escorting additional friends of Walt's, a Mr. and Mrs. Eduardo Prieto and their two daughters from Mexico City. They were to be given top treatment, including lunch at the Red Wagon Inn and, of course, the afternoon show at the Golden Horseshoe. As we walked towards Tomorrowland, one of our new attractions was nearing completion. It was the Astro Jet, a new thrill ride that consisted of several small one-man rockets. These rockets would fly around in a large circle and the pilots could make their rocket go up and down as they made their loop. Another attraction, an aerial tram ride that ran between Fantasyland and Tomorrowland, was called the Skyway and was about to begin trial runs.

DISNEYLAND, INC.

INTER-OFFICE COMMUNICATION
10-02A 5M 9-55 CP

Date___March 22, 1956____

To_____Bob d'Arcy_____   From___Bev Palombo_____

Subject_____

This is to confirm arrangements made with you this morning.

Mr. & Mrs. Eduardo Prieto and two daughters will arrive
between 11:00 A.M. and 12:00 Noon, tomorrow. They are special
friends of Walt's and he wants them to have "Top Treatment",
lunch including. You are to stay with them at all times.
They will ask for you upon their arrival at Main Gate.

Bev

MAR 23 1956

MAKING SURE everything was set for the Prietos' visit.

During lunch, I mentioned to Mr. Prieto of my plans to study at the University of Mexico and he offered me a place to stay. In addition, he offered to assist me in any way he could, as he was an attorney and had many valuable contacts. Between Mr. Prieto and the Maestro Stokowski, I felt like I was building a reserve of valuable contacts for my dream of studying in Mexico City.

After lunch, we took the girls on all the rides in Fantasyland and then we were off to Frontierland. They really enjoyed the Mark Twain, but I could not wait until our arrival at the Golden Horseshoe. We took our seats in the usual stage left box. The show had not yet begun. Jimmy Clark was playing the piano and doing his warm-up routine. My guests mentioned that Walt had told them about the show and they were waiting with great anticipation for it to begin. When Jimmy finished, the trio took their places in the orchestra pit and began playing the opening theme. The chorus girls were very colorful and their dancing set the pace of the show. Don Novis added his usual class and his singing of the turn-of-the-century songs created the mood of that era. Wally Boag was quite humorous with his dialogue and I remember one line in particular:

"You will be reading about me in the newspapers; I smoke in bed." It always got a big laugh, and he was very clever with his balloons. When Judy appeared, I purposely watched the looks on my guests' faces, and they brightened up. She did this to everyone. Now, that is charisma! When she came over to us with her usual pretty bow, the look she gave me was so warm that my thoughts turned to the time when we would meet and go to her home for another lovely evening.

Easter Sunday was a most beautiful day. The weather was ideal for our first Easter Egg Hunt, bright and sunny, with a nice turnout of guests. Many children were eager to find the Golden Egg and enjoy a day at the park with Walt. I spent part of the morning with Dad at the Maxwell House having coffee and visiting with some of the guests. I had two tours booked for the afternoon so I spent the rest of the morning in Adventureland at the Bazaar, sharing some tea with Davey Lee.

My first tour was with a lovely woman named Lil Steele. She was the ex-wife of Al Steele, the President and CEO of Pepsi-Cola, who had recently wed Joan Crawford, the actress. This was one of those tours where you became friends as opposed to just being the tour guide. She had many interesting questions about the park, and inquired about me and my future plans. We had many laughs. When I escorted her to the Main Gate, she said, "Why don't you take a trip to New York and let me show you around?" I replied that I would enjoy that immensely and she gave me her address. One of the great things about my job was not only meeting such interesting people, but also getting invitations to visit them where they lived and worked, places I had never been.

My next tour was a shorter one and I returned to my office around 4:00 P.M. About ten minutes later, I received a call from a switchboard operator, who said, "Bob, I have a very angry man on the line. I have tried to locate the executives who could talk to him, but no one is in their office. Could you please talk with him and find out what is troubling him?" I took the call and to say he was angry would be putting it mildly. He was livid! He said, "I demand to talk to Walt Disney! If not him, then the next person in command. I have never been so upset in all my life and I don't know who you are, but if you can't do anything about this situation, I'll find a higher source." He proceeded to rant and rave as I stumbled to try to calm him down and determine what had happened. He finally said, "I drove a long distance to bring my five-year-old son to Disneyland and I told him about the Easter Egg Hunt. I explained to him that if he found the Golden Egg, he would have a tour of the whole park with Walt Disney. When I told him that, his face lit up and that was all that was on his mind. I put my son in the group with the rest of the children and watched them happily crawling around searching for the eggs. As I saw him about to grab the Golden Egg that he had just spied, one of your executives pushed his child in front of mine and he grabbed the Golden Egg. My son was so disappointed, he cried for some time." I asked him who the executive was and he replied that he did not know. After my son calmed down, I assured him that I would pursue this matter further, as we were both extremely upset and I know Walt Disney would be upset as well.

I was not too surprised when I found out who the executive was: Tommy Walker. Now I was the angry one and I went over to see Dad. Since this confrontation had landed on my lap, I was anxious to find a satisfactory resolution to this incident. As I related the story to Dad, he asked what I planned to do. I told him that I intended to relay the incident directly to Walt.

"That's not a good idea, Laddie. Drop this on someone else's desk and let them handle it." I protested, "But Dad, if this man decides to make an issue of this and it reaches the newspapers, it could hurt Walt. Besides, it was a rotten thing for Tommy to do. I'm not interested in causing trouble for Tommy. I care about Walt."

He replied, "Son, I know how you feel and I would probably feel the same way, but you understand how Walt is when it comes to someone telling him about a wrong someone else has committed. Give it to someone higher up and hope that justice will prevail."

I knew Dad was right when I left him. I was so brought down

by all of this that I took a long walk and thought of how I would feel if I were that father. But, even more, I felt so bad for that little boy and how disappointed he must have been. If I were the father, I might have strangled Tommy.

I returned to my office, called Jack Sayers' secretary, and relayed the events to her. As head of Guest Relations, Jack should handle the situation. I never knew what became of that incident, but I hope that Walt had been informed and he had done something nice for that little boy. Nothing changed as far as Tommy was concerned. He was still the head of Customer Relations and his child had the Golden Egg. The one thing that continued to baffle me, however, was how did that man know that Tommy was a park executive?

It was around this time that Bob Jani told me he was getting married. The wedding was going to be in San Francisco and he would like to have Judy and me attend. I told Judy and she was excited about the upcoming trip to San Francisco. The time was just right as Judy had some time off and I had no problem getting a few days off myself. I gave a lot of thought as to what to give Bob for a wedding gift. Knowing that he would be receiving most of the usual wedding gifts, I remembered a very large, beautiful, black-and-white photograph of the castle given to me by Fritz Musser, one of Disneyland's first photographers. This would make a great gift, because Bob loved the park and I knew he did not have any pictures of it. I only wished the photograph had been in color. Then I remembered my dear Mother, in her younger days, used to be what they then called a portrait tinter. This meant she would use oil paint to give photographs color, as most photos in the 1920s were black and white. I gave her the castle picture and she did a magnificent job that truly brought the picture to life. When framed, it greatly enhanced its size and subject.

Judy and I loved San Francisco and we had a wonderful time. The wedding was nicely done and the castle gift was a big hit. One evening, we all met at the Papagayo Room in the Fairmont Hotel. We enjoyed one of the best Mexican meals I had ever eaten. This was one of Dorothy Manes' favorite hangouts from her old days

DISNEYLAND, INC.

INTER-OFFICE COMMUNICATION
FORM 10-02A 10M 12-55 OCPCo

DATE 4/3/56

TO   ERWIN VERITY   FROM   ED ETTINGER

SUBJECT   VICE ADMIRAL RICHMOND

Confirming our telephone conversation, we will expect Vice Admiral
Richmond, his staff, and members of the Senate Appropriations Committee at Disneyland at approximately 3 p.m. Saturday next.

Arrangements will be made to meet this group at the entrance to
Disneyland and to guide them through the park.

We have also made arrangements at the Gourmet Restaurant at the
Disneyland Hotel for cocktails at 6 p.m. to be followed by dinner
at 7:00.

We will await details on the names of this group.

Many thanks.

EDE:jpa

CC: Joe Fowler; Dolores Voght; Ed Hack; Tommy Walker

PLANS for the arrival of Vice Admiral Richmond.

living in the Bay Area. With the many margaritas we all consumed,
it was a joyous evening.

After the celebrations concluded, we returned home via the
coastal route, Highway 1, one of my favorite drives from Northern
California to the Southland.

Back at work, I had a high profile tour from the Pentagon—
Coast Guard commandant Vice Admiral Richmond, his staff, and
members of the Senate Appropriations Committee. They were on
a very tight schedule, and I had to show them highlights of the park
in 45 minutes. I was able to accomplish this by using the service
road and, knowing the ticket takers, being admitted to the head of
the lines. The group enjoyed the Jungle Cruise, the Mark Twain,
Storybook Land, and finally a trip on the Disneyland Railroad,
which ended at the Main Gate. I then escorted them to the
Disneyland Hotel, where they enjoyed a cocktail party and dinner.

10

Walt wanted a circus to be a part of the park—a huge tent, three-ringed stages with animals, clowns, high-wire acts, the whole works—but the cost and space needed was too much to deal with on a continuous basis. So after staging a Mickey Mouse Club Circus for seven weeks through Christmas, he decided to hold over one of the most popular acts from the circus, Professor George Keller. George Keller's act was unique in that he had a mixture of big cats. There were two African lions (one named Leo), one mountain lion, one panther, two tigers, and a cheetah. A very large circular cage made of steel pickets housed his act, with bleachers outside for the audience. He had two assistants working with him, one at each end of the cage with loaded rifles ready to shoot if he were in imminent danger. It was quite fascinating to watch him work, as he did not use a whip, a chair, or a handgun, only white gloves. George would talk to the cats and, at the same time, move his gloved hands in a rhythmical way that seemed to have a hypnotic effect on them. He put each cat through its act and at the end of the performance, the cats would all exit... except for Leo, who sat on a stool near the exit. George would come up very close to Leo and yell for him to leave. Leo would take a swipe at George with his large paw, just missing him, before he would slowly make his exit. Leo would then stop, give George a nasty sneer, and growl before he would finally leave, ending the show.

I escorted many guests to view George's show and they were continually entertained. Some guests were genuinely afraid that Leo, at the end of the act, would attack George. When I would have a lull in my schedule, I would often catch the show on my own. On one occasion, I introduced myself to George and asked him a few questions: "Do you ever get scared or have an unsure feeling when you are in the middle of those dangerous animals?" He answered, "No. If they sense any fear you might be feeling, you are in trouble. That is the first thing I learned when I began working with domestic cats as a young boy at the age of ten. I was fascinated by cats at that very young age and became interested in big cats when I would attend the circus." I then asked about the white gloves and he replied, "Cats are color blind and the gloves appear bright to them, so I am able to keep their attention and put them in a mild trance."

When I questioned him about the end of the act, the scary part with Leo, he said, "I used to go up to him and pry his mouth open and stick my head in a little way, but he has changed as he has gotten older, so I altered his routine to swipe at me instead." He was very proud to have his show at Disneyland, as he was a big fan of Walt's portrayal of animals. "Disneyland is one place I was hoping to perform; now my dream is to take my show to Madison Square Garden in New York," he said.

George was with us for about seven months and then he hit the road. Evidently, about four years later, he died in the cage of a heart attack. But I didn't learn of his demise until many years later, reading about it in a magazine. According to the fanciful article, he died under far grislier circumstances. At the end of one performance, Leo attacked him and with one swipe of his powerful paw, George allegedly was decapitated. His head flew out of the iron cage, and his body lay motionless. All of the cats jumped over him and made their exit, just like every other performance. I recall one thing he told me was that "You always have to be ready for the unexpected, because you never know what is on their mind."

However, with Judy and me, it was very clear what was on our minds. We were very much in love. My brother Ron found a lovely woman who worked for Dad at the Maxwell House and my old friend, Larry Alves, met his Miss Beverly, who worked under him at the Pavilion. They not only fell in love, they were married and are still together at this writing. Ah, the Magic Kingdom.

Judy and I were frequently invited to parties and, on many

occasions, when there was a piano present, we were often asked to perform a couple of tunes. I loved working with her, but I was limited in my musical ability. To back a great singer, you have to have a working knowledge of music, such as how to sight read all the many chords and how they progress. You need to be familiar with a vast number of songs in all the keys. In addition, you must be able to anticipate the singer's moods as to how she is interpreting a particular song. In spite of all the techniques I did not know, she never made me feel that my lack of ability was an issue. She actually made me sound much better than I actually was. She continually encouraged learning and for me to keep working; how could you not love such a "for real" woman?

The first accident that I recall in the park was during the stagecoach ride through the Painted Desert in Frontierland. A grandmother and her grandson were the only occupants in the stagecoach when it suddenly flipped over on its side and finally slid to a stop. Those five-eighths scale horses were known to spook easily. On this day, during the ride someone had dropped a small paper cup in the horses' path and they freaked out, catching the driver by surprise. The passengers were shook up, but fortunately were not seriously injured. They had a few cuts and bruises, which First Aid attended to before sending the injured guests on to a nearby hospital. En route, I asked them how they were feeling and the grandmother said they were fine. The grandmother recounted, "I heard that Walt Disney wanted the attraction to be realistic, so when we tipped over, I thought that was a part of the ride and we were being chased by Indians."

Cornell Borchers was a big screen star in Europe during the 1950s. Publicity called me and said she was working on a film at Universal Studios and was taking a break to visit Disneyland for a picture layout to publicize her visit to America. This was my first assignment of this nature, part tour and photo session for a movie studio. She arrived with a publicity man named Louis Blaine. Cornell was a gorgeous blond woman in her late 20's, dressed in a

GERMAN ACTRESS Cornell Borchers visited the park, with a Universal Studios cameraman close at hand.

European-style white coat, scarf and gloves. She reminded me of Ingrid Bergman, one of my favorite actresses who starred in the classic movie *Casablanca* with Humphrey Bogart. We strolled down Main Street, stopping to take photos of her at the Penny Arcade for a shot, then on to the Hub to photograph her with the castle in the background.

As we made our way through the different Lands, she would

MARK TWAIN was the perfect photo spot.

occasionally put her arm through mine as though we were on a date. There is something about having a beautiful woman locked in your arm that pumps up your ego and makes you feel proud to be who you are. I could see envy in the eyes of some of my co-workers as, by now, they realized what a great job I had.

Cornell attracted attention everywhere we went. We boarded the Mark Twain to take more pictures, and she made the ship look even more magnificent, as she stood on the bow, waving at the guests.

We took a break for lunch, and she asked me many questions about the park and many more about Walt Disney. She was overwhelmed with the beauty of the park, especially the many different architectural designs.

When the photo shoot was completed, we ended at the railroad station where I was flattered by Cornell asking to have a picture taken with me. What a sweet lady, and one of my most enjoyable experiences as Disneyland's first host. I claim this prestigious title because I was the host to many people during the construction phase of the park, and because of my knowledge of every aspect of its development. I was given the job as a Guest Relations assistant, which of course deals with introducing and escorting special guests throughout the park.

11

Rita Hayworth was a huge movie star of the Forties and Fifties, and a real beauty. At that time, she was in a relationship with Dick Haymes, who was a fine singer in competition with Frank Sinatra. They were to arrive around 11:00 A.M. I met them at the front gate and I was a little concerned about this tour as it was obvious they were already "feeling no pain" after having had a few cocktails en route to the park. They must have been forewarned that no alcohol was served at Disneyland, so they prepared themselves ahead of time for the tour.

They were not drunk, but they did not walk in a sure-footed manner either. I introduced myself; they acknowledged me and, from that point on, it was as if I did not even exist. They were completely hung up on each other. I wondered if they really wanted to be at Disneyland at all. It seemed to me that the publicity people at her studio set the tour up, but there was no one to accompany them. As I walked them up Main Street and approached the Hub, I said that maybe they would like to tour the park on their own and they were quite happy to do so.

I left them and returned to my office. I phoned security and alerted them of our "spirited guests," should any trouble arise. It has been said that "variety is the spice of life," and that was certainly proving to be correct as far as the tours I was experiencing at the park.

My next tour was taking the Russian press and their interpreter through the park. It was a treat for them that their boss, Nikita Khrushchev, with all of his power, could not match. They were a happy group of men and eager to know all about the park. They were especially interested in what Walt Disney was all about. Going

DELEGATION of Russian journalists was dazzled by Disneyland.

down Main Street, I pointed out Walt's apartment and they mentioned that they would like to visit it. I told them that I was not authorized to take guests on a tour of it, even ones as special as they were at the time. We arrived at the Hub, which they thought was a most interesting concept, having all the Lands spinning off it. We proceeded on to Tomorrowland and into the Circarama, which they thought was fascinating, as they had never seen anything like it before. We completed our visit of Tomorrowland and continued on to Fantasyland. As was usual with my tours, they stopped and were in awe of the castle. We must have stood there for ten minutes, with them asking if Walt had designed the castle, how long it took to construct, was it real inside, and did the drawbridge really go up and down. It had become almost predictable that every guest I escorted through the park would stop and marvel at the sight of it. Once inside, they recognized Dumbo and thoroughly enjoyed Storybook Land. We continued around the Hub and into Frontierland, where Sheriff Lucky and Black Bart were doing battle. We stopped and caught the whole routine; the Russians got the biggest kick out of it, and I introduced them to the cast. The Mark Twain dazzled them and they all had a turn at the wheel in the pilot's cabin. Unfortunately, there was not time on their schedule to take in the Horseshoe, but they did get a peek of it in progress.

Adventureland, as always, was a big hit and the animated animals provoked many questions, as did the Zulu warriors. We ended up at the Carnation Ice Cream Parlor for a banana split. During this treat, I was asked questions about Walt. "What kind of man is he?" I replied that if Walt had met them at the front gate instead of me and taken them on the tour, it would have been pretty much the same. He would have been more interesting because of who he was, but just a real, down-to-earth person, who enjoyed life and didn't appear to realize what a genius he was. They were amazed at my description of Walt.

We said goodbye at the front gate and they thanked me for all my information about the park and Walt Disney. Weeks later, I heard from Walt's office that the Russian contingent was impressed with my knowledge of the park and with my enthusiasm. Despite the language and culture barriers, they understood everything I was saying. What a compliment!

My day was almost over, so I went to the Horseshoe to catch the last show of the day. After the performance, as Mel, Judy and I were leaving Frontierland, we stopped at the Hub. I asked Mel if he had to leave right away. He said, "No. Why?" I pointed to the castle and said, "There is the best place to have a 'poke' in the whole park."

He chuckled and said, "How do we get in there?" I told them to wait and I would get the key and be right back. Once inside

VIP GUESTS included Dorothy Page, secretary to the Federal Communications Commissioner.

Fantasyland, we went to the left side of the castle, and down to the end where we found a small door. The door was difficult to see, as it blended in with the castle's color scheme. No guests were in this area and, as we entered, we used our cigarette lighters to illuminate the stairs as we climbed to the top. Our seating area, at the top window, consisted of two sawhorses and a small plank of wood. The carpenters had left the materials there to be used later when the interior decorators and set builders would create the story of Sleeping Beauty. It would become a colorful interior attraction.

We had a "poke" and sat in silence, looking at the park from this private view. We could see Tomorrowland, Main Street, Adventureland and Frontierland all lit up. It really was a memorable sight. We sat for a while, had some great laughs, and left. Mel said goodbye, and Judy and I departed for her house. I put on some music while Judy fixed drinks. We sat on the couch, relaxed and did some serious music listening, making for just another loving evening with a beautiful lady.

The next morning I was up early, around 7:00 A.M., when there was a knock at the back door. Judy said, "Get that for me, Love." I opened the door and it was a guy named Gordon from the wardrobe department. When he saw me at the door, the look on his face was a mixture of shock and horror, then disappointment, as he was expecting Judy. He said, "Where is Judy?" I advised him that she wasn't ready yet and he grumbled, "Tell her to come in early, she has a fitting." Poor Gordon, he was expecting to fit Judy in the privacy of her home.

One of my favorite actors of all time was James Stewart. Such films as *Mr. Smith Goes to Washington, It's a Wonderful Life, Rear Window, Vertigo, The Naked Spur, Winchester 73, Call Northside 777, Bend of the River,* and *The Glenn Miller Story* were some I remember the most, and now I was about to meet this great star and his lovely wife, Gloria, on their first visit to Disneyland. What impressed me the most about him in his movies was his sincerity. He always cared about the little guy and was a true example of the American hero. I met them and talked about the railroad station and explained that most of Disneyland was built to a five-eighths scale, and to be sure and take the train ride around the park. He was just as nice in person as he was in his movies, and Gloria was much like him.

We walked up Main Street, which he remarked looked very much like the towns in which he had grown up. When we arrived at the Hub, I pointed out the various lands and asked if they would like me to stay with them or continue on their own. He said, "Mr.

D'Arcy, you have been a wonderful host, and the two of us would like to see the park together." He shook my hand and gave me a warm thank you. This was one tour that I would have certainly enjoyed continuing. They were such nice people and Jimmy was very interesting to talk with. I could sense, however, when guests wanted to continue by themselves. I told them to have a great visit and, if they needed anything at all, I would be at the Police Station to assist them.

12

Nobody knew Blinky better than Mel and I did. When we wanted to have a "poke," Blinky's domain was the perfect place. It was out of the public's eye and there was never anyone around. Mel dropped by the office one day when Barbara was out to lunch. We left by way of the back door and headed down the service road to visit Blinky. When we arrived, we could not believe what we saw. There had always been a bucket hanging on a hook connected to Blinky's mechanical base, which would be full of rags. The maintenance crew would use these rags to wipe the grease from their hands after working the gears that brought life to Blinky. This particular day, the bucket was void of the usual rags. In place of the rags, there was a ladies bra and a pair of panties. As we both cracked up at the discovery, we noticed that the grass was missing from Blinky's mouth and he had nothing to chew. We proceeded to have a "poke," and as we laughed at the sight of Blinky's empty mouth, we suddenly thought of a solution. When Blinky swung around, out of sight from the guests taking the ride, Mel held his long neck while I hooked the bra and panties into his mouth. Letting him go, Blinky continued his long swoop back into view of the guests. The timing was beautiful. At that moment a boat full of guests was approaching and the startled boat driver spieled, "And there, folks, is old Blinky the giraffe. Well, I'll be darned if I know where he found that in the jungle, but he must have had a good time." The uproarious laughter from the guests could be heard throughout Adventureland. Mel and I were hysterical and barely made it back to the office. We were out of control, sides aching, tears rolling out of our eyes, when the phone rang. I could barely stop laughing long enough to answer it. "Hello, Bob. This is Sergeant Pace from security, and we have an emergency. Somebody put a woman's bra and panties in Blinky's mouth. Watch out for someone running around the service road. If Walt hears about this, there will be big trouble."

I said, "Slow down, a bra and panties in Blinky's mouth? How could that have happened?" He went on to say, "I don't know, we have had our security force out looking for whoever did this." I said, "That is disgusting. I'll sure keep a watch out for anybody suspicious around here." I do not know how Mel contained himself during this conversation, but as soon as I hung up, we lapsed into uncontrollable laughter. We were finally able to contain ourselves just as Barbara returned from lunch. Mel said hello to her and left. It was difficult to relate to Barbara the phone call from Sergeant Pace, as I fell into yet another laughing attack. She joined in my laughter and, before long, the whole park had heard about Blinky's new diet. Just the vision of the bra and panties in Blinky's mouth flopping in the breeze would send me into another laughing frenzy. I have often wondered who had been involved in the "hanky panky" and why the woman would leave her underwear behind. Years later, Mel would call me from his and Ann's lovely home in Carmel, California, and tell me how he had related the Blinky story to their guests and would inevitably have them laughing hysterically. Mel and I had immortalized Blinky.

The following morning when I arrived at my office, I started to crack up once again at the thought of Blinky. Then it suddenly occurred to me that I could be the prime suspect in that bizarre caper due to the location of my office, as well as my connection to the previous party in Walt's private apartment. The weekend brought Walt out and as he approached me, he just smiled and said, "How is everything going, Kid?" I replied that it was great and he proceeded on to his apartment upstairs. He never mentioned the incident with Blinky, nor did he even hint at any suspicions he might have had about the incident. As time went by, I never heard anything from Dolores or anyone else at the Studio.

The Thirties, Forties and Fifties were the Golden Era of popular

American music. Never in our history have we had so many prolific composers and lyricists in just three decades. Such masters as Harold Arlen, Irving Berlin, Duke Ellington, Jerome Kern, George Gershwin, Cole Porter, Richard Rodgers, and one of the greatest in this distinguished group, Frank Loesser. It was my privilege to meet Frank and escort him around Disneyland. He was unique, like Cole Porter and Irving Berlin, in that he wrote the music as well as the lyrics to most of his songs and Broadway shows. His hit Broadway musicals included *Where's Charley, Guys and Dolls, The Most Happy Fella, Greenwillow,* and *How to Succeed in Business Without Really Trying.* Among his song hits were "Heart and Soul," "Two Sleepy People," "On a Slow Boat to China," "I Don't Want to Walk Without You," and "Spring Will Be a Little Late This Year." He also wrote the words and music to the World War II big hit "Praise the Lord and Pass the Ammunition."

Frank and his lovely wife and children flew out from New York for their visit to the park. The minute I met them, I knew they were high-class people, well dressed and the children were very sharp and well mannered. We took the train ride around the park first, and Frank was impressed by the authentic look of the train and Main Street. In his early days, he had lived in California, was on the music staff of Universal and Paramount Studios, and had seen many movie sets.

After a slow walk up Main Street, we stopped at the Hub, and once the children saw the castle, they led us to Fantasyland, where they took in every ride. When the kids were about to take the dark rides, I escorted Frank and his wife to Storybook Land. They really enjoyed the ride overall, especially the miniature Black Forest.

After the kids had had their fill of Fantasyland, it was on to Frontierland and down to the dock to catch the Mark Twain, which impressed them greatly. I escorted them up to the pilot's cabin where the kids all took a turn at the wheel and received a pilot's license. I was hoping my brother Ron would be captain, but another employee was on duty—a very nice fellow, but not as colorful as Captain Ron.

We caught the early show at the Horseshoe. Frank was very entertained and had great things to say about the colorful production and, especially, the music. This particular show was a highlight not only for my guests, but for me as well. Charles Lavere, the piano part of the trio, had just written a new song for the show. It was called "Riverboat Blues." Judy's interpretation was very soulful and she really brought the song to life.

As I sat with my guests and listened to the new tune, I thought how apropos for to be listening to a new tune for the first time in the presence of a great composer, an experience he enjoyed many times for many shows on Broadway. He thought Judy was a fine singer, so after the show I introduced Frank to the band. He shared some laughs with Mel and complimented the men on their performance. I wanted him to meet Judy, but she had to change clothes and we were due at the Red Wagon Inn shortly for lunch.

We dined at the Red Wagon in Walt's private dining room. As soon as we were seated, Frank said, "I heard Walt does not serve liquor in the park, so I brought my flask of scotch. Is it OK for me to mix in the privacy of his room?" I said, "Sure, if you share it with me!" He had a good laugh over this and we mixed our drinks and made a toast to Walt and a memorable visit to Disneyland. During our feast, I told Frank how much I enjoyed his music and shows and that I was in the process of learning one of his songs that I liked a lot, titled "If I Were a Bell."

He asked if I was a musician and I replied that I was just beginning to study the piano seriously, and when I mentioned the Lighthouse and the musicians I was studying with, he was familiar with some of them, namely Shorty Rogers, my buddy who taught me how to play the trumpet, which enabled me to get into the Army band. Frank then questioned my future plans. I told him that I had hoped to study in Mexico, indicating that it would be cheaper to live and study there. He said, "Would you consider studying in New York?" I replied that I had not considered that possibility, as I knew New York was a very expensive place to live. He replied, "I have my own publishing house. You could work for me and I could

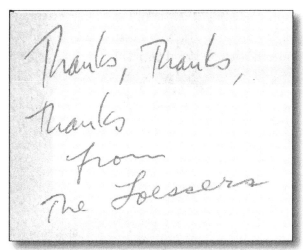

THIS THANK YOU card from Frank Loesser and family made me a Most Happy Fella.

set up living quarters. I know some great teachers you could study with, and I can show you how to get around and meet people who could help you in the business." I was overwhelmed by his generous offer and said I would give it a lot of thought, as it would make a huge change in my life. He said, "Take your time, and if you decide to come east, let me know."

After lunch, we took in the Jungle Cruise and the Loessers thoroughly enjoyed it. Midway through the ride, when Blinky popped up, I started to laugh. Frank asked what was so funny, so I said, "If we get a chance, I'll tell you." We never did, since I could not relate that story to his wife and children.

It was into the evening when we completed our tour. We had a nice farewell chat before they departed the park. There are some visits you do not want to end and this was definitely one of them. We all hugged and they left with a final wave.

About two weeks later, I received a small package in the mail. When I opened it there was a gold, slim style Dunhill Executive cigarette lighter with a simple, lovely note that read, "Thanks, Thanks, Thanks, The Loessers." What a show of class from some very down home people. I still have that beautiful lighter and the fond memories of a bright day in my life. I never took Frank up on his offer, as my life took a different course after Disneyland. I have often wondered where I would be at this time in my life had I gone east.

13

Life was just terrific. I had the greatest job. I was in love with a fabulous woman. I was meeting great friends and beginning to sit in on jazz jam sessions at the piano. I was definitely climbing to a high point, and enjoying it immensely. Then a dark cloud slowly started to cover me.

Every morning, during my workweek, Dad would wake me up to have breakfast, prepare to go to the park, get to my office, and have another great day of work. Mother would have the table set, fresh coffee ready, and we would all enjoy a pleasant morning together. This morning was very different.

Dad woke me up early, before the rest of the family, and said, "Get up, Son. I have to talk to you about a serious matter." By the tone of his voice, I knew he was a little upset. When I got to the kitchen, I poured a cup of coffee and sat down at the table. He began the conversation by asking, "Do you smoke marijuana?" I replied, "Yes, Dad, I do."

He continued, "I'm glad you are truthful, because your Mother and I found your supply in your bedroom closet." I said, "Who told you of this?"

"Mark Stevens," he replied. Mark Stevens was the Chief of Police of Santa Ana. I met Mark, a nice man, during the early days of the opening of the park. I told him that any time he or his friends wanted to visit the park, to call me, which he did on several occasions. I would leave special press passes at the gate in his name. Dad went on to say, "He called me yesterday afternoon and made a dinner date, saying he had to have a serious conversation with me. At dinner, he advised me that someone had informed him that me, Mel and Judy had smoked the 'herb at the park.'" "Why was someone always squealing on me?" I thought.

Mark went on to say, "I think Bob is a fine young man, but I don't know Mel or Judy. From my observations of the show at the Horseshoe, they seem like nice people, and I do not want to see them in any trouble with the law. I especially don't want to see Bob becoming involved in any scandal." He concluded, "Jim, I am not angry or upset by this. I see it all the time and this is my only warning to them. Please advise them to clean up and be very careful in the future!" I thanked Dad for being so understanding and not getting all shook up about this incident.

He said, "Son, why do people smoke marijuana?" To which I replied, "Why do people have a martini or a couple of glasses of wine? I enjoy the relaxing feeling it gives me. It does not make you crazy or cause you to do violent things; it just makes you hungry, and you sure do laugh a lot. It's always a very positive and happy experience."

He replied, "Well, be that as it may, watch your step and tell Mel and Judy to do the same." I assured him I would convey the message and for him not to worry. We would not smoke it in the park any longer, and we didn't.

As I drove to work, I thought how lucky I was that Mark was not your usual police chief who would have reveled in making a nice drug bust at a famous park attraction, thus putting a big feather in his hat, and how fortunate to have loving parents who truly cared about my well being.

When I arrived at my office, I called Mark and related my conversation with Dad. I told him how much I appreciated his concern for us and I took his warning seriously and thanked him for his understanding. How relieved I was. What I did not understand at the time was why the informer called Mark instead of the police chief of Anaheim. He would have been the logical contact to call, since he was closer to life in the park. Whatever the reason, Mel, Judy and I were grateful that the informant's call went to Mark.

Long before Judy and I got together, she was dating a fellow named Sonny. I never knew his full name, but she had told me about their relationship and that she had endured a minor problem after their separation. He was the type of guy who would not accept losing her and did not want anyone else to have her love. When he learned that Judy had found another boyfriend, he could not deal with it. One day, while Judy was at work, he broke into her house, closed everything up tight, turned on the gas stove without lighting the burners, and proceeded to begin the act of suicide. After a short while, he decided to have one last cigarette and, as he struck the match, a mild explosion occurred and a small fire started. He panicked and, as his clothing caught fire, he ran outside, catching the attention of the neighbors, who called the fire department. It was not very long before the press arrived and the next day the story was made public.

One of Disneyland's first scandals was born. Sonny's burns were mild. He was charged with breaking and entering and attempted arson, and was subsequently arrested. Judy was quite upset about this unfortunate incident and, for a time, it made her life complicated from questioning by the police, bad publicity, people at the park bothering her with questions, and everyone wanting to know the full story.

Disneyland was not at all happy about this incident, especially Walt and Tommy Walker, since he was in charge of all talent in the park. Judy had told me of some of her encounters with Walker and she never felt comfortable around him. He had hinted that he would like to have an affair with her. This was one of the reasons he did not care much for me, especially since it was well known that Judy and I were serious about each other.

Not long after her ordeal, Judy was summoned to the studio for a meeting with Walt Disney. He said that, as much as he liked her personally and admired her talent as a singer, the incident had put an undesirable mark on the image of Disneyland and, therefore, he regretfully had to dismiss her. I have always believed that Tommy Walker was influential in Walt's final decision. That night, after her meeting with Walt, we were at her house and she was understandably upset about losing her job. Not only did she love the show, Mel and everyone else involved with it, she truly loved Walt and being a part of Disneyland. Moreover, it was steady work for a singer and, as she said, "I will have to move back to Hollywood and stay with Mom until I find a job." This would entail meeting with her agent and going on endless interviews in search of work.

Judy's replacement was a woman named Betty Taylor. She was attractive and a good singer, but nothing like Judy, who had charisma and radiant beauty, as well as being a more soulful performer. To me, there really was only one Slue Foot Sue and that was Judy Marsh.

It is a sad feeling when your once-happy life is on an upward surge and suddenly starts to tumble on a downward plunge. Judy's absence from the show was difficult enough, but not seeing her on a daily basis, including our special nights together, began to take a personal toll on me. I now saw the park in a different light, and it was getting dimmer. That special sparkle that I always felt about Disneyland was slowly fading. My tours were beginning to become routine and, when I escorted my guests to the Horseshoe, if it were not for Mel and the band, I think I would have bypassed the Horseshoe and continued with the tours.

Since I was on a six-day work schedule, my one day off was a drive to Hollywood to be with Judy. Her mom was a great lady by the name of Harriet. She had a loving but firm personality. Yet when it came to Judy, she acted almost like a manager, not only of Judy's career, but of her personal life as well. Fortunately, she liked me and we became good friends. Judy's stepfather lived with Harriet and was a very interesting man. He was the retired Vice President of Columbia Records, who formed and developed their Country Western Division, called Western Swing Music. In those early days, he discovered Gene Autry who, at the time, was a hard-drinking, down-and-out nobody. Arthur Satherley was his name, but to western music fans and country stars, he was known as Uncle Art, the "silver-haired granddaddy of western music." He made Autry a huge star and businessman, who would eventually own radio and television stations, a publishing house, and the California Angels baseball franchise. Roy Acuff was another big western star who had found fame through Arthur Satherley. Art and I had many interesting conversations about music and the workings of the music industry.

The park was slowly changing for me. Besides Judy's absence, Dad had finished his career at the Maxwell House and had moved on to new ventures. Some money people in Arizona, who owned the famed Apache Junction, which was located at the foot of Superstition Mountain, contacted him. Apache Junction consisted of a restaurant, bar and a small zoo, and a lot of land with picturesque views of the mountains and lush desert vegetation. Dad was asked to develop the complex to resemble Frontierland, only in a much grander scale. One of the featured attractions was a large saloon with liquor and real dancing girls who would approach the customers and actually have a drink with them. There was a much larger restaurant, motel, enlarged zoo and an "ole swimming hole" for the kids, plus rides and exhibitions. Everything was designed to look and feel as if it was actually the Old West. Due to Dad's poor health, however, this venture never materialized and he moved back to California.

I really missed going to the Maxwell House, having coffee with Dad, and discussing the current events happening in the park. Many employees missed holding court with him, as he was one of the first originals to leave Disneyland.

14

Walt once said, "Disneyland will never be completed," and that was proving to be true. As Disneyland's second summer began, Tomorrowland's new ride, the Astro Jet, was in full operation and was a big hit with the teenagers and young adults.

New additions to Frontierland and Fantasyland opened to much greater fanfare. On June 16, 1956, a modern day Tom Sawyer and Becky Thatcher dedicated Tom Sawyer Island, officially opening the park's newest development. The youngsters we used were Chris Winkler (Tom), who was 12 years old, and Perva Lou Smith (Becky), who was 13 years old. They arrived by airplane from Hannibal, Missouri, bringing with them a box of soil from Jackson's Island in Hannibal, and bottles of water from the Mississippi River. They won their titles in an annual statewide contest in Missouri and were selected by the Hannibal Chamber of Commerce.

The two Mark Twain characters planted the box of soil at the foot of the island pier and christened the Tom Sawyer rafts with the bottles of Mississippi River water. They were neat little touches of authenticity that gave Walt a big smile.

Bob Jani planned the itinerary for the dedication and, along with Bob, the public relations staff, my hosts and hostesses, and I gave tours of the island to special guests and visiting dignitaries. The island had many features that were in the original *Tom Sawyer* book.

The path to Fort Wilderness was dotted with large boulders that had been brought to the island in landing craft vehicles because some of the massive rocks weighed as much as seven tons each. Fort Wilderness had its lookout towers, a canteen, and a trading post offering apple cider. The fort was a real log replica of the frontier outpost in use at the time of Daniel Boone.

TOM SAWYER Island under heavy construction.

The island itself was a "walk-through" type exhibit. Visitors climbed Lookout Peak and toured Injun Joe's Cave. Inside the cave were tunnels leading to rooms hung with dripping stalactites. The floor opened to show a gaping bottomless pit from which cold air blew up from an unknown source. The cave's interior was decorated to carry out the story of Injun Joe's secret hiding place from the Huckleberry Finn and Tom Sawyer stories.

At Lookout Peak, one could see the burning settler's cabin and, in yet another area, a deserted Indian village. Wild animals were seen all around the island—elk, moose, deer and mountain lions fashioned from lifelike plastic.

One could take a path leading to a suspension bridge, another dirt walkway just for strolling, or another route that led to a point

SKYWAY gondola ride, built in Switzerland and imported to the U.S. by Disney, linked Tomorrowland to Fantasyland.

where you could see a beautiful vista of the Mark Twain with Frontierland in the background, an excellent spot to take pictures.

After touring the island, we all boarded the newly christened rafts to return to the Plantation House terrace for a fish fry luncheon. The entertainment was provided by Disneyland's very own Dixieland band.

The following week, on June 23, the spotlight shifted to Fantasyland's new ride, the Skyway. Since it was constructed much like the ski lifts prominent in Switzerland, Walt wanted the entire Los Angeles Swiss consulate to participate in the opening ceremonies.

I met the dignitaries at the front gate at about 10:00 A.M. and led them up Main Street into Fantasyland and up the chalet stairs

GIVING A TOUR of Fantasyland to the wild and crazy engineers who worked on the Skyway.

to the landing where you would board the gondola ride. Counting the members of the consulate, our publicity staff, and me, there were about 20 of us waiting for Walt to give his dedication speech to a large group of guests gathered below. Walt made his way up to

ANOTHER STOP for the Skyway engineers was the Davy Crockett Arcade. Note Dad in the background, over my left shoulder.

the microphone to stand in front of us, with me behind him and to his right. For some reason, when looking at him and the crowd below, I was reminded of a funny scene from the movie *The Great Dictator* with Charlie Chaplin, which made me feel a huge laugh forming inside of me. At that moment, Walt, with his mustache, looked like the Chaplin character. I wanted to laugh so hard; I had to really struggle to compose myself. Could you imagine what would have happened if I had let out a burst of laughter in the silence just before Walt began his speech? It seemed like hours before he finished and we all took the ride to Tomorrowland, two passengers in each "bucket," as we called the vehicles on the ride. I was in the fourth bucket; Walt was in the first. Thank God, because that laughter finally burst out of me. A nice gal from publicity was with me and I could not tell her what I was laughing at until we

THE MINE TRAIN through Rainbow Ridge was another big addition to the park in 1956 and another opportunity for Disney's designers to use forced perspective.

had reached Tomorrowland.

Everything went as planned for the dedication and after we landed in Tomorrowland, we all went to the Red Wagon Inn for lunch. Everyone was seated at the large table in Walt's private dining room, except for three seats at the head of the table. Walt had not arrived yet and Ed Ettinger, the head of publicity, said, "Bob, you take the end chair, I'll sit next to you in the middle, and Walt will take the last seat." Well, Ed waited for Walt before he sat down and when Walt came in, he immediately sat right next to me and Ed wound up sitting on the end chair. Walt said, "Hi, Kid," and I said, "Hi, Walt." Just looking at him so close, that big laugh started to brew big time once again inside of me. I excused myself to the men's room and once outside of the dining room, I burst out laughing once again to the puzzled look on the faces of the restaurant staff. I was finally able to join the lunch party.

15

My hosts and hostesses handled most of the tours and I stayed with the VIP's and special guests, as I was requested to do by Walt's office or the publicity department. I retained my good spirits, but inside I was suffering a slight depression—a feeling that I had not experienced before. My happy times were with Mel and other good friends. At night, I was going with Mel to some of his music gigs, which helped to fill the void of not being with my love, Judy. I was also getting some gigs of my own and they too helped me in coping with the loss of Judy and with the changes taking place at the park. Then one night, coming home from a gig, it all came crashing down on me. I parked in front of our house and started to cry. I did not try to stop it by trying to be brave. I just let it flow and finally the tears came to a stop. I was totally drained. I had hit the bottom.

Judy was getting work in town and was busier than ever. Sometimes our one night together consisted of a short meeting at the Fog Cutter, a neat, small Polynesian-style tiki bar in Hollywood. When she finally got her own apartment, that helped keep our relationship alive. However, a long distance relationship begins to take its toll, and the long drive took up a lot of the time we could have spent together. I could not stay overnight, as I would have to rise very early in the morning to get to work on time, leaving me with very little sleep. Because I was not sufficiently developed musically, this element was slowly beginning to separate us more. It used to frustrate me that during our one day a week together, I would drive her to a friend's house, who was a fine musician and piano player, to rehearse her in putting together her new nightclub act. That I was unable to be a part of something so close to us both started to hurt.

I continued to enjoy my work, but it was becoming more of a chore than the job it once had been. My good friend Bob Jani was going to leave, but not because of changes in the park. He was being drafted into the Army. We had a nice meeting before he left and I advised him of the traps to avoid when he started Army life. After he completed basic training, he was stationed in Mineral Wells, Texas. We stayed in touch and I kept him informed of the events happening at Disneyland.

Things were going along fairly smoothly until Tommy Walker, once again, had to mess things up. One morning, he called me to his office and said, "Bob, I think it would look better if you wore the same uniform as your hosts and hostesses." I questioned his reasoning and he replied that he felt it would make our department appear more organized. What a phony cop out. What he was doing, in actuality, was demoting me, as every department head dressed in their own clothes, even the ride operator supervisors did not wear a uniform. Moreover, I had received many compliments on my attire. I said, "I do not feel that is right and I do not like uniforms." He said, "Well, we'll see about that."

A few weeks later, when I drove to Hollywood to see Judy, I made one of the toughest decisions in my life. We were having a nice evening together, when I told her I could not take this schedule any longer and I felt it would be easier if we parted company. She was a little taken back by this and said, "I felt this coming on, as well, and maybe we should just get married."

I said, "I would love that, but since we are on different levels career-wise, it would be a rough road to travel. Before long, it looks like you will be going on the road with a band soon, and long separations would damage our relationship." She agreed with me, and with a gut-wrenching last hug, she said, "Christmas is almost here. Will you come and spend some of the holidays with me?" I replied, "I don't know at this time what the folks have planned or where I'll be, but we will keep in touch." With one last warm kiss and tight hug, I told her goodbye.

On the drive home, again came the tears. I am such a

sentimentalist. When I was very young, my dear father used to call me "Bladder Eyes" because whenever anything sad happened, it would prompt me to start crying. (Even now as I'm starting to write this beautiful story, I have to keep stopping and grabbing Kleenex, just thinking about all the fond memories and all these lovely people who are now all gone.) I knew I would never see Judy again; it would be too painful. I braced myself for a long recovery.

The next day when I arrived at my office, Barbara informed me that we would have to vacate the office for a half-hour or so. The Mouseketeers were coming to the park to participate in a special event and the studio had requested that we let them change into their costumes in my office. Our location was closer to the event than the wardrobe department, so my office, for the first time, became a dressing room. I felt it was due to Tommy Walker trying to, once again, lower my status. Something was telling me that it was time to move on. About a week later, I gave Tommy my two-weeks notice. I was leaving my great job and the "kingdom" I loved so much.

On my last day as Disneyland's first host, I walked the whole park and halfway through I stopped, thinking of Dad, Mother and me making this same walk on the eve of Opening Day. That vision took me back to my first day when I began this great adventure almost two years earlier. I recalled that first drive to the studio with Dad, then on to the "site" a week later to start being part of Walt's dream. I truly loved the beginning as much as I did hosting the many guests who shared my love of this baby of Walt's never-ending creative mind. The aroma of new timber, fresh paint, all new vegetation, seeing real gas street lights installed in a modern era, a castle being built, a five-eighths scale world, complete with its own railroad, stagecoaches from the Old West, even five-eighths scale horses, a real riverboat, built from scratch, complete with a real steam engine, and even a jungle with "real" animated animals. I stopped at the entrance to Frontierland and thought of all the preparation that went on before the big television broadcast, how I peeked into the Horseshoe and caught my first glimpse of Judy and the band.

I stopped at the Horseshoe and waited for the show to end. When it was over, Mel and I went to the Carnation Ice Cream Parlor for our last lunch together in the park. We ordered, and Mel asked, "What are your plans now, man?" I told him of Dad's Arizona connection, but before he started that project, he was hired as a consultant by the big candy and restaurant chain named Albert Sheetz. They had a large restaurant and bar in Long Beach, California, and Dad hired me and my trio to handle the entertainment and music. Mel was happy for me and wished me luck. We made a vow to stay in touch.

I left Mel and went into my office for the last time. I gathered my personal effects from my desk and said goodbye to Barbara. I headed to the old administration building area parking section, climbed into my MG, and left the park.

I decided to take a drive down to the coast, via those roads that were still unaffected by progress, taking in the orange groves, the avocado groves, and quaint farmhouses. For a short time, I thought back to when Judy and I took this same route in happier times. Then, thinking of the park, I realized how very blessed I was to have experienced such a fantastic part of American history. I slowly started to feel proud, as only a few people could say that, and I suddenly felt a surge of happiness coming over me, thinking about the first time I met Walt, and the many encounters in between. I reminded myself that many people would have been thrilled just to see him up close.

The only regret I had regarding Walt was that I should have requested a short meeting with him at the studio, which he would have granted me. I would have told him, "Since I no longer work for Disneyland, much to my regret, I want to warn you about Tommy Walker. Now, I know, Walt, that you do not like snitchers, but I am not a snitcher; I am a concerned friend. I am so grateful to have been a part of the park and the chance to know you, being a friend. I do care about you, so just watch out, and be aware of his moves."

I do not know how he would have regarded my sincere meeting with him, but I do know he would have thanked me for it later on. I would later learn from an old musician friend from the early days that Tommy pulled a shady deal in the early development of Walt Disney World, purchasing valuable land for himself in Florida near Walt's secret site.

I reached Newport Beach, parked the car, and took a long walk on the beach. Thinking of my last two years with Disneyland, I realized how beautiful the whole experience was, and that it was definitely time to move on to my music career. I could forget the pain of not having Disneyland in my life, but the pain of not having Judy in my life was another matter.

16

After Disneyland, I first played jazz piano for my father's new restaurant, the Squires Inn in Long Beach. But I soon found myself working regularly in television, thanks to a couple of assistant directors—my Uncle Harry and his son, Bill. Through the 1960s, I worked steady as a stand-in and stunt double, most prominently for Bob Denver on *Gilligan's Island*, but also frequently on *Combat* and *Bonanza*. Starting in the 1970s, I moved primarily to feature film work, first as a stand-in for George Burns in *The Sunshine Boys*. Fittingly, my final film was for Disney, *The Rocketeer* (1991). I was hired for the bit part of a short order cook, but ended up also appearing as Adolph Hiltler.

Through it all, I never forgot my Judy. In 2003, her lovely daughter, also named Judy, set up a surprise meeting. The moment we were reunited, our eyes locked in, and laughter and love once again bloomed as we shared a long warm hug. She was still as beautiful as ever. Unfortunately, she had suffered a stroke a few years earlier and could not speak, but we still communicated through pure love.

A couple of years later, on my birthday in 2006, I was playing piano in a jazz trio with a bass player, Michael Oletta, who shared the same special day. So Bryan, our sax player, and my youngest son, Eric, planned a special birthday celebration for us at Disneyland: one more "walk in the park." As we set foot on Main Street, my mind was flooded with fond memories. As we stood at the entrance to the Police Station, my old office, I told my friends about the rear entrance to the service road and all about Blinky. They all cracked up. As we looked at the Fire Station, I shared about Walt's private apartment and my infamous party.

YOUR HOST
HOST
The Pleasure
Guide

BOB D'ARCY, latest progressive jazz
pianist, making his local debut at
SQUIRE'S INN.

RESTAURANTS

DINING-DANCING

ENTERTAINMENT

AMUSEMENTS

WEEK OF OCTOBER 26, 1956

Published Every Week by
EDWARD G. WHEELER
18192 Lillian Way, Tustin, California
Phone Kimberly 7-2978
6   Copyright 1956

MY FIRST professional gig was playing jazz piano at my father's new restaurant, the Squire's Inn in Long Beach.

ONE OF MY most memorable roles was as a robot in an episode of *Gilligan's Island*.

MY LAST ROLE was as Der Fuehrer in Disney's *The Rocketeer*.

ALONGSIDE artist/writer Dave Stevens, creator of *The Rocketeer*.

I led them to Adventureland, which had changed a lot and become much more crowded than in 1955. I told them I had a part in "staking the track" that the boats ride on.

We entered Frontierland and I stopped them at the Golden Horseshoe and peeked in to see the show in progress. It was totally different from the original—no lovely ladies, all male comics. I then took them to the Mark Twain for a ride, then it was off to Fantasyland. As we approached the castle, my mind recalled that special evening when Mel, Judy and I sat on a sawhorse at the very top room for our private nighttime viewing of Disneyland. We took in some rides and after we walked through Tomorrowland and

SO EXCITED to see an old friend when I finally returned to Disneyland in 2006.

wound up at the Hub, where I really liked the statue of Walt and Mickey that had been added. We found a park bench and sat down, as I continued sharing what it was like when I first saw this magnificent dream of Walt's all come to life.

Once a tour guide, always a tour guide... and I loved every minute of it!

Index